**Praises for *Lietuvybė Down Under***

'This work confronts and bridges a gulf of misunderstanding, indifference and suspicion, left in the wake of the Cold War thaw, with a loving care and respect for her subjects and a passion for the rigour of her work.'
– Josef Šeštokas, author of *Welcome to Little Europe: displaced persons and the North Camp*, 2010

'Extremely well researched, very well written ... Regarding my parents' generation, it was interesting to read that shortly after arriving in Australia some believed that there might be another war and that they might be able to return relatively quickly to a free Lithuania. Remembering my father's discussions, he never believed this and thought that people who did were naive.'
– John Mašanauskas, *Herald Sun*'s journalist, Melbourne

'This book has highlighted the complexity of the issues regarding identity for those members of the Baltic communities who wish to maintain links with their respective cultural traditions.'
– Dr Ojārs Greste, Sydney Latvian Community

'well written and valuable'.
– Dr Nathan Hollier, Director, Monash University Publishing

## *Also by Grazina Pranauskas*

Pranauskienė, G *Eukaliptų tyloj* (In the silence of eucalypts), ŽŪIKVC spaustuvė, Vilnius, Lithuania, 2007.
Pranauskienė, G *Abu krantai* (Both shores), Eglės spaustuvė, Klaipėda, Lithuania, 2011.
Since 1997 published in various Deakin Literary Society Anthologies, Geelong, Australia.
In 2017 and 2018 her short stories have been published in the multidisciplinary peer-reviewed journal *Lituanus*, Chicago, Illinois, USA.

# Lietuvybė Down Under

## Maintaining Lithuanian national and cultural identity in Australia

GRAZINA PRANAUSKAS

Australian Scholarly

First published 2018 by
Australian Scholarly Publishing Pty Ltd
7 Lt Lothian St Nth, North Melbourne, Vic 3051
Tel: 03 9329 6963 / Fax: 03 9329 5452
enquiry@scholarly.info / www.scholarly.info

ISBN 978-1-925801-17-0



*Cover design:* Wayne Saunders
*Cover photo:* Demonstration of three Baltic states, Adelaide, 1989

*To the Centennial of the Restoration of the State of Lithuania*

# Contents

# Acknowledgements

This is a book based on my BA (Honours) thesis 'Fifty years of Lithuanian culture in Australia 1940s–1990s' (1998), and my MA by research thesis 'National and cultural identity in diaspora: a study of Australian Lithuanians' (2003).

My sincere thanks to all who contributed to this publication whether it be correcting it or giving valuable comments. Without the assistance of Professor Algimantas Taškūnas (OAM), Dr Egidijus Vareikis, Alena Karazijienė (OAM), Dr Uldis Ozolins, Dr Ojārs Greste, Josef Šeštokas, John Mašanauskas, Dr Aldis L. Putniņš, Nimity James, Terrie Fraser, Jane Berkley, Catherine Malcolm, Liliana Braumberger, and Irena Grinkaitė this project could not have been completed.

I am grateful to Professor Algimantas Taškūnas (OAM), Daina Pocius, Dalia Doniela, Žydrė Pember, Algimantas Žižiūnas, and Aldona Scano for providing images to enrich the book. Also to Sue Opulskis for images and her initial suggestion to call my publication *Lietuvybė down under.*

My special thanks to Professor Ron Adams for editing *Lietuvybė down under* and for his enormous dedication to the Lithuanian community in Australia.

Most importantly, I thank my husband Peter for his patience and moral support during the years leading to publication of this book.

I would like to express my gratitude to the Australian Lithuanian Foundation for supporting this project.

# Prologue

> The word *lietuvybė is* difficult to translate, because it has somewhat different meanings for different people. *Lietuvybė* may be seen by some as the sum total of everything Lithuanian, including the nation's culture, traditions and language. Others believe that *lietuvybė* is, first and foremost, a measure of a person's ability to speak Lithuanian. There are quite a few other variations on this theme, as well.
>
> Algimantas Taškūnas (ed.), *Lithuanian Papers* no. 26, 2012

The meaning of *lietuvybė* has shifted for me in recent years. When I arrived in Australia in 1989 and was becoming part of the Lithuanian community here, I had no doubt that the most important aspect of *lietuvybė* was the ability to communicate in the Lithuanian language. But I soon discovered that confining *lietuvybė* to language excludes many people of Lithuanian descent – like my husband Peter – who do not have a command of the language but passionately identify as Lithuanian. I have had to rethink what it is that makes people like him proud of being Lithuanian. What makes him become emotional when listening to Lithuanian singing. Content when eating Lithuanian food. What drives him to place Lithuanian ornaments around the house. Plaster our car with Lithuanian stickers – even when he is not sure of the exact meaning of the words.

Although belonging to a later generation of Lithuanian migrants to Australia, I have for a long time been fascinated by the postwar refugee generation's understanding of *lietuvybė*. When I arrived in Australia, I knew virtually nothing about them – and why they were regarded as traitors of the

Soviet Union by the Soviet-era propaganda. I set myself the task of listening to the stories, not only of the surviving refugees and their struggle to preserve a 'pure' Lithuanian identity free from foreign influence, but also of their descendants who (like my husband) may not have retained the language, and more recent arrivals who (like me) grew up in the Soviet era. What I have learnt is that each of us has our own concept of *lietuvybė*, but that we also share two important characteristics in common: we all identify as Lithuanian, and we all live outside the homeland.

What I have come to appreciate more and more since 1989 is that living in the diaspora poses a continuing challenge in terms of maintaining an authentic concept of *lietuvybė* unsupported by the implicit affirmation that comes with living in the homeland. Ironically, I hardly use Lithuanian today, as I work in an English-speaking environment – even my research into the Australian Lithuanian community's national and cultural identity is written in English. Initially, the language shift worried me. But now I feel a sense of pride that I am able, even in a miniscule way, to contribute to the maintenance of *lietuvybė* by stepping outside the Australian Lithuanian community in order to promote it to current and future generations of Australians.

Much of what I have learnt about *lietuvybė* is based on interviews I conducted with community members in Sydney, Adelaide, Geelong, Hobart and Melbourne from February to October 1998 for a BA Honours thesis, and from questionnaire returns and interviews with leaders and members of the different Australian Lithuanian organisations in the same cities from October 1999 to January 2000 for an MA thesis.[1] That research informs this book. The book is not intended to be the last word on what *lietuvybė* has meant to succeeding generations of Australian Lithuanians – life is far too dynamic and fluid for there ever to be a last word! – but Chapters 1–5 do give voice to a representative cross-section of the community in terms of gender, date of arrival, age, geographical spread and educational background.

Chapter 6 is different. It steps away from the voices of others and gives expression to my own voice. It is not the researcher voice of Chapters 1–5. It is my novelist voice, with extracts from my PhD novel 'Torn: the story of a Lithuanian migrant'. Its inclusion acknowledges that analysis can capture only so much – and in this respect it is telling that when Australian Lithuanians talk about *lietuvybė* their talk is not analytical and objective, but descriptive and personal. So too Chapter 6, which is intended to pay homage to *all* the stories told – and stories yet-to-be-told – by countless members of the Lithuanian community in Australia.

# Introduction

I arrived in Australia in September 1989, five months before Lithuania proclaimed its independence from the Soviet Union. I soon learnt that Lithuanians living here closely identified with the 'Lithuanian community' – a central force, as I later found, in the lives of many postwar migrants. I was pleasantly surprised that Lithuanians in Australia spoke the Lithuanian language, and that community activities such as Australian Lithuanian Days were organised on a regular basis.

I felt welcomed by the Lithuanian community in Geelong, of which I was part from May 1990 to December 1998. Local Lithuanians embraced me for my professional choral conducting skills and for founding the Lithuanian choir Viltis (Hope). Although initially pleased by this constant attention, as I adjusted from being a *guest* to being a *local* Lithuanian, I began to realise just *how* different I was from other Lithuanians in Geelong. I began to see that other Lithuanian migrants in Australia perceived Lithuanian national and cultural identity very differently from Lithuanians in Lithuania – who did not have the same need to 'preserve'[1] their identity.

In time I discovered that people identifying as Lithuanians in Australia can be divided into three distinct groups: post-World War II Lithuanian migrants, their descendants, and second wave or more recent arrivals who started to settle here from 1970. The first postwar Lithuanian migrants were Displaced Person (DPs), refugees from war-torn Europe. In this book I treat all postwar Lithuanian migrants who arrived between 1947 and 1960 as first-generation migrants. Their descendants, who identify to varying degrees as Lithuanian, Lithuanian Australian or Australian Lithuanian, are categorised as second or third generation Lithuanians. The views of *their* descendants, children of the Australian-born generation, are different again in terms of what they tell us about the current situation of Lithuanian activities and how Lithuanian national and cultural identity might be expressed in the near future.

My own family experiences, like those of many other Lithuanians during World War II, share features with those of postwar Lithuanian migrants. My maternal grandparents fled their home with their family at the end of the war and found refuge in war-torn Germany. But in contrast to Lithuanians who emigrated overseas, my grandmother chose to return to Lithuania with her four daughters after the war. On the way to dig German trenches, my grandfather escaped back to Lithuania, where he went into hiding until the end of the war. In the 1950s he was interrogated by Komitet Gosudarstvennoy Bezopasnosti (Committee for State Security, or KGB) agents as to why he had fled Lithuania, and whether he was a spy. Released without charge, he lived into his 90s.

I felt a strong affinity with other second wave Lithuanian migrants who had settled in Australia in the 1980s. At the same time, I admired the descendants of postwar Lithuanian migrants for their sense of personal freedom, their ability to communicate in English, and their command (often partial) of Lithuanian. I sometimes thought that if my grandparents had come to Australia in the late 1940s, I would have been part of that group. After more than 28 years in Australia, I am still on a mission to discover my own identity – a journey that intersects with similar journeys by other Lithuanian Australians. In 1998 I documented part of the journey in a BA Honours thesis: 'Fifty years of Lithuanian culture in Australia 1940s–1990s'. I expanded on the journey in 2003 with my MA thesis: 'National and cultural identity in diaspora: a study of Australian Lithuanians'. More than a decade on the journey continues. Like many Australian Lithuanians, today I live with a sense of a divided self, of rootlessness and cultural anxiety – and this current book may be read as my latest attempt to articulate what it means to live in the 'in-between'[2] cultural space we call Australian Lithuanian.

For many Australian Lithuanians living in the liminal space we associate with a diaspora,[3] existence is experienced as living 'on the periphery of power, or excluded from sharing power.[4] Like millions of other 'displaced peoples and dislocated cultures' that have moved from 'settled communities' into the new ways of life of the diaspora, we have had to adjust to new historical realities, new uses of language and new meanings of citizenship – where we are never far from feeling displacement and cultural dislocation.[5] In such sites of displacement and of separation from the homeland, communities select and preserve cultural traditions in a new hybrid environment. With modern technologies such as air travel, telephones and, increasingly social media, we find ourselves in a border relationship with the 'old' country. The new technologies provide a way of bridging the geographical and psychological gap between host country and homeland, but life in a diaspora is still – well, *diasporic*.[6] Conditions of life remain for many of us an experience of dispersal and alienation, with the memories we cling to fanning the desire for eventual return 'home'. Some will never return, believing 'there is no homeland to which to return.' Others return only to discover that it has changed so dramatically that it is no longer the 'welcoming place' they remember,[7] with people and their attitudes simply unrecognisable.

We will see in the chapters that follow what it has meant to postwar Lithuanian migrants, their descendants and second wave Lithuanian migrants to occupy different diasporic spaces: the postwar generation with their memories of an independent Lithuania, their Australian-born descendants who often find themselves locked in battle with older members of the community over what they see as an 'old-fashioned' identity that their parents and grandparents want to preserve, and the second wave generation who came to Australia with a political and cultural outlook shaped by the Soviet era. What they have in common is the urge to avoid cultural rootlessness and the need to impose meaning on the world.

With such differences within the community, is it even accurate to talk of 'Australian Lithuanian culture'? The notion that 'no culture can be measured or evaluated against another'[8] would seem to apply as much to differences *within* the Australian Lithuanian community as to differences with other groups. 'A group's culture', Ann Katrin Eckermann has observed, 'is relevant only to its own particular group.' It helps to 'determine how people of that group perceive themselves, how they conceptualise or order their world, what propositions or beliefs they use to explain things, how they try to cope with their world as well as the sentiments and values which tell them what is good and what is bad …'[9] As I have discovered, the observation applies to divisions *between* Australian Lithuanians as much – if not more – than what divides them from other Australians.

As we shall see, the assimilation policy of the 1950s did not help Lithuanians to become part of mainstream Australia; rather it prevented them from integrating with other Australians. Like other newcomers, they experienced ethnic tensions. Referred to as 'New Australians', 'DPs', and 'Balts', made them feel like 'outsiders'. Nonetheless, they generally regarded Australians as fairly neutral in their attitudes toward them, and some Baltic migrants were themselves ethnocentric and maintained a social distance, including being against mixed marriages between themselves and Australians.[10] Many Lithuanians felt safer keeping their distance from the mainstream and mixing with their own people.

Forced to flee their homeland after the horrors of war, and geographically detached from their past, postwar Lithuanians had to rely on their memories to recreate the traditions of their homeland. Different lifestyles, a different climate, and above all the vast distance from the homeland, created a *new* Lithuanian culture in Australia. This new culture differed significantly from that of their homeland – just as the evolving culture within the borders of Lithuania differed so much from the patterns of the past. Lithuanians on both sides of the globe continued their traditions, but in both cases recontextualised and redefined according to changing circumstances.

There is little point judging if one is more 'authentic' than the other. All we can say is that Australia's postwar Lithuanians tried valiantly to preserve what they perceived to be authentic, ancient homeland traditions, by reshaping and adjusting them under the guidance of a dedicated cadre of community leaders. As this book describes, the challenge was to 'restage' core aspects of Lithuanian culture in the alien environment, with community leaders choreographing cultural gatherings to preserve what they judged to be important cultural traditions, like dancing and singing. As we shall see, they were forced to adjust their cultural practices. To take a small example: in order to make national costumes, Lithuanians replaced woven woollen skirts and linen blouses with dresses made of materials better suited to the Australian climate. In the same way, they incorporated Australian ingredients into their national food.[11]

The changes and continuities in *Lietuvybė down under* over a 50-year period are explored in the chapters that follow. We shall see that claims about *this* or *that* expression of culture as the only authentic or legitimate expression of what it is to be Lithuanian in Australia inevitably express personal value judgements. We are, after all, not talking about an abstract culture, but *real* people trying to deal with issues of divided self, rootlessness and cultural anxiety. And we are not just talking about individuals: the quest for identity, the journey towards self-realisation, was not undertaken by individuals acting in isolation. They were social acts, undertaken with others and, while not exactly the same, each person's story intersects with similar journeys undertaken by others.

The two primary elements of shared identification were language and ethnicity.[12] But these elements were not immutably fixed. In my own case my ethnic origin is Lithuanian – my parents and grandparents on both sides were Lithuanian. My husband's father's parents and grandparents were Lithuanian, and the relatives on his mother's side were Irish, and his ethnic origin is Australian. He does not speak Lithuanian, but he considers himself Lithuanian.[13] What this shows is that people 'recognise' themselves in and relate to similar life experiences, and on this basis share a particular identity. The identity is related to culture – the ways of thinking, values, customs and traditions of a particular social group with which a person identifies. This means that 'identity' can – and does – change in line with changing socio-political and material circumstances. One sociologist has referred to identity as a 'changing illusion'.[14] Another refers to it as a 'moveable feast'.[15] Whatever the metaphor, it is clear that as life's circumstances change identity shifts, dislocating or decentring a stable sense of self.

From this perspective, identity should not be seen as an already accomplished or completed 'production', but always something in the process of becoming – always constituted within, not outside, representation. According to this view, the very notion of an authentic 'cultural identity', tying inseparably identity and culture, which cannot exist without each other, is problematic. People with a shared history and ancestry share a cultural identity formed and shaped under the particular circumstances of their existence. Cultural identity reflects, then, not only the past but also the future. It is not just something that already exists. It comes from particular histories as they unfold – particular life stories as they are told – constantly transforming from one moment to the next, even when transformation is resisted and denied, as has been the case among Australian Lithuanians.[16]

Given this constant transformation, cultures cannot escape a continuing process of hybridisation – an evolving mixture of old and new, them and us, meanings and discourses, giving rise to something new and often unrecognisable, and leading to continuing negotiation of meaning and representation. A collective group of migrants exposed to a new living environment may strive to preserve its national and cultural identity, but in a diaspora the identity necessarily varies from that of the homeland, with cultural representation constantly being 'translated' into the lived environment. Inevitably the result is hybridised meanings.[17]

As this book describes, Lithuanian identity in Australia has been exposed to this kind of hybridisation over the past 50 years, with postwar refugees and more recent migrants bringing to Australia distinct 'symbol-forming activities'[18] traceable back to their different-era lives in the 'homeland'. In both cases, new historical, political and cultural developments in the diaspora transformed previous identities into hybridised versions, continually drawing from (changing) memories of the homeland and experiences within the host society. This renders 'pure' identity a fiction, a myth, with national identity trying to follow 'tradition' not so much inherited as 'invented' – reflections of past experiences in present circumstances.[19] This is not to deny that many of the postwar Lithuanians in Australia have clung tenaciously to a preserved identity, have attempted to quarantine it from the new environment – in the belief that, if not preserved in the diaspora, Lithuanian culture would be lost. So too many later arrivals have held onto what they identified with as Lithuanians. The identities are different: the process is much the same.

Other authors have explored the issue of preservation of national and cultural Lithuanian identity in the diaspora. Authors of Lithuanian descent, such as Liucija Baskauskas and Monica Baltutis, have discussed how Lithuanians, in common with other ethnic diasporic minorities, were exposed to unavoidable mainstream assimilation. The American Lithuanian Liucija Baskauskas has examined the ways in which postwar Lithuanian migrants in the United States have dealt with assimilation within a pluralist society where they blended in and became invisible.[20] In Australia, Monica Baltutis has investigated the effect of intermarriage between postwar and second generation Lithuanians and non-Lithuanians.[21] Like Baskauskas in the United States, she concludes that assimilation into the mainstream is unavoidable. I am not so sure. 'Assimilation', where the ethnic group and the host group become 'virtually indistinguishable'[22] is perhaps too strong a term. It overlooks how the host society is itself in a constant state of transformation and, like diasporic communities, is subject to a process of hybridisation.

To the postwar Lithuanian generation, remaining visible in their host country meant being ambassador for Lithuania, responsible for its image and for the maintenance of the Lithuanian language. For their descendants, visibility is being in-touch with what their parents and grandparents would regard as secondary aspects of culture. But if we accept that notions of 'pure' culture are fictions and myths, 'being in touch' – even in ways that others might regard as diluted – is just as authentic an expression of cultural identity.

CHAPTER 1

# Constructing 'Lithuania'

## *Second millennium BC–1939*

The sense of a divided self and rootlessness among Lithuanians in Australia was exacerbated by living in a diaspora. But it has its roots in Lithuania. The 'homeland' itself was never immune from cultural shifts and accompanying cultural anxiety. The shifts were particularly pronounced following the outbreak of World War II, as Lithuania lurched from independent statehood to Soviet occupation, to German rule, to Soviet reoccupation, to post-Soviet independence. In providing an overview of these shifts and their impact on Lithuanian identity, this chapter draws from the works of many other writers – some of whom are unashamedly partisan.[1] But even the most partisan accounts offer insights into the worldview that postwar Lithuanian refugees and later migrants brought with them to Australia.

That worldview was fundamentally different from the Soviet school curriculum that was drummed into me in my formative years. I grew up oblivious to how my schooling either ignored or distorted Lithuanian history. Lithuanians of my generation never learnt that the formation of Indo-European proto-nations in the Baltic area can be dated to as early as the second millennium BC, or that in 1040 AD 'Lithuanians' existed as a tribe. We knew nothing of the Slavic attempts to colonise the eastern Balts between the fifth and the eleventh centuries, of how the eastern border stretched from Pskov to Minsk by the twelfth century, with only a few of the Baltic enclaves remaining unassimilated.[2]

Under the Soviet system, Lithuanians of my generation were denied the opportunity to study the written sources that showed how our history as a nation began in the thirteen century, with the fight for national freedom continuing for 750 years. As school children we were never allowed to experience the sense of pride of earlier generations in how the Lithuanian state was established in 1219. Or in how the Grand Duchy of Lithuania united in 1236 by Grand Duke Mindaugas (later crowned King of Lithuania) survived for some 500 years. Or in how, during the fourteenth century reign of Grand Duke Gediminas, Lithuania expanded south to the Dnieper and Bug rivers, with Gediminas assuming the title of King of Lithuania and a large part of Russia.[3] As if the Russians would have allowed us to reflect on Gediminas as King of Lithuania *and a large part of Russia*!

Only much later did I begin to learn about Gediminas and his achievements, such as the founding of Vilnius as capital of Lithuania. It was only after I arrived in Australia and started to read the accounts of mainly expatriate Lithuanians that I began to understand the reasons behind the chequered history of Lithuania's struggle for a separate national and cultural identity. How, after the expansion of the Lithuanian state in the fourteenth century, between two-thirds and three-quarters of its people were Russians. How the Lithuanian army, legal system, administration and finance were all organised on the Russian model. How Rhutenian (or Old Belarussian) became the official language of the new state ruled by the Grand Prince Algirdas. How, although geographically Lithuania became the largest European state, Lithuanians were outnumbered by Slavs. How nonetheless the indigenous Russian and Ukrainian populations were dominated by Lithuanian aristocratic landowners. How in 1362 the Lithuanian army under Gediminas' son Algirdas crushed the Tatars and Mongols in the Battle of the Blue Waters. And how the cost of these constant battles with its neighbours was that Lithuania had to align itself with Poles, leading to the formation of a Polish Lithuanian state at the end of the fourteenth century.[4]

All of this – and more – was known by the postwar Australian Lithuanian generation. Dates of which I knew nothing were etched in their minds: 1377, when the death of the Lithuanian Grand Prince Algirdas began the association between Poland and Lithuania; 1385, when Grand Duke Jogaila issued a declaration known as the Krėva Union Act marking the beginning of Polonisation in Lithuania; 1386, when paganism ostensibly came to an end, with Lithuania the last European country to accept Christianity the following year – though pagan elements associated with nature continued to be reflected in national customs and traditions; 1410, when the united Lithuanian Polish army defeated the Teutonic Order, stopping Germanisation of Eastern Europe; 1547–84, when Ivan the Terrible took much of the Lithuanian and Tatar lands and proclaimed himself Tsar of all the Russias.[5] For me and my Soviet-era generation, reciting such dates was tantamount to disloyalty to the state. For the postwar Australian Lithuanian generation, it was a way of remembering that they were part of a venerable tradition of forging and maintaining a distinctive Lithuanian identity.

When they came to Australia they brought with them what they had learnt as school-children in the 1920s and '30s, when Lithuania was free and independent. How, in order to defend themselves, the Lithuanian rulers relied on Polish military forces, accepting the Union of Lublin in 1569 and ending the independent history of the Lithuanian principality. How, although Polish influence lasted over 400 years, the Lithuanians were not 'subordinated' by the Poles, but kept their own Court (as a Grand Duchy), lands, institutions and army.[6] How in 1579 Vilnius Academy-University was established with faculties of philosophy and theology and, although the language of instruction was Latin, subjects taught in Lithuanian – as well as Byelorussian and Polish, with the number of Lithuanian, Polish, Byelorussian, German, Swedish and Hungarian students increasing from 700 to 900 in ten years and the University becoming the cultural centre of Eastern Europe and helping to raise Lithuanian educational standards.[7]

The University might be viewed as a metaphor for the evolution of Lithuanian national and cultural identity – a 'moveable feast' in the words of Stuart Hall, constantly absorbing influences of other cultures.[8] Lithuanian identity has never been 'pure', but has always been intermixed with the identities of other nations. Yet, despite being a moveable feast, there did emerge a distinctive Lithuanian national and cultural identity with which people could identify, and with which the postwar generation *did* identify. Of course, like any identification, it's a social construction, but in terms of people's self-identity no less real for that.

The identity is embedded in language. The Lithuanian language developed around the fourth and the third centuries BC, making it 'the oldest surviving language of the Indo-European group' according to philologist Theodore S. Thurston, with its own distinctive morphologies, archaic sound systems, and lexical features.[9]

What the postwar generation would have recognised as 'modern' Lithuanian national culture has its origins in the sixteenth century. In 1547 the author of the first Lithuanian book, the Rev. Martynas Mažvydas, published a *Protestant catechism* for Lithuanians living in Prussia, on the grounds that a book in their native language was the most effective tool to discourage them from believing in pagan gods. In 1599, Canon Mikalojus Daukša expressed his concern in *Postile* (Postilla catholicka) that the Lithuanian tongue had become greatly Polonised, and urged the Polonised nobility 'not to forsake or disdain the tongue of their forbearers', and for Lithuanians by birth not to feel ashamed of their native language.[10] Nations, he argued, do not survive 'because of their soil's fertility, the diversity of their clothing or the strength of their cities and fortresses, but primarily by preserving and using their own language which increases and sustains a common foundation, harmony and brotherly love.'[11]

A hundred years later (1697), Polish became Lithuania's official language, replacing Old Slavic for written communication. But Lithuanian authors continued to address their nationals in the native tongue, and in the 1760s the Protestant pastor Kristijonas Donelaitis wrote the first literary work *Metai* (The Seasons), which became a Lithuanian classic after its publication in 1818. Such publications were significant in shaping Lithuanians' sense of themselves as a distinct nation, which was still being expressed and celebrated a century and a half later among the postwar refugees arriving in Australia.[12]

Throughout its history, Lithuanian identity was largely defined in opposition to foreign rule. In the second half of the eighteenth century (1772, 1792 and 1795) the Polish Lithuanian Commonwealth was divided into three partitions, ruled over by the Russian empire, the Habsburg Austria and the Kingdom of Prussia. While Russia, Austria and Prussia divided up the Commonwealth lands among themselves, seizures ensured that territorial boundaries were shifting and changing. By the end of the eighteenth century Lithuania was governed by Russia and the Lithuanian population exposed to Russification, though, reflecting the Polonisation of the Lithuanian nobility, the Polish language initially was tolerated. During the years of Tsarist occupation (1795–1915), Lithuanians were forced to assimilate and convert to the Orthodox faith. After 1861 schooling in Lithuanian and the use of the Latin alphabet were prohibited, as well as the publishing, possessing or reading of Lithuanian books. Following the failed Polish and Lithuanian insurrection of 1863, Polish-speaking teachers were replaced by unqualified Russians, the Polish language was banned in the education system, and all official correspondence was carried out in Russian.[13]

But Lithuanian resistance continued through the written word. In the 1880s Lithuanian nationals risked their lives to smuggle the first Lithuanian newspapers *Aušra* (The Dawn) and *Varpas* (The Bell) from Prussia into Lithuania. Those caught possessing publications were beaten, tortured and exiled to Siberia, but people hid books in haystacks, churches and even cemeteries. Between 1891 and 1902, Russian customs seized more than 170,000 Lithuanian books and publications smuggled from Prussia, but those that did get through nourished an underground education program and contributed to a growing level of literacy among Lithuanians.[14] While smuggled in and distributed by the 'secular intelligentsia', the publications are credited with not only nurturing 'Catholicism and Lithuanian ethnicity', but with helping to give rise to a 'Catholic Lithuanian nation'.[15] In Australia all those years later, postwar Lithuanian refugees still identified with this anti-Russian resistance and embraced as their sacred duty the need to maintain and defend the Catholic Lithuanian nation in exile.

Looking to the past was one way of bolstering their confidence that ultimately they would prevail. Many could remember the lifting of the prohibition of the Lithuanian press in 1904, and the Tsarist 'proclamation of freedom of consciousness', which had allowed Lithuanians to return from Russian Orthodoxy to Catholicism. Religious education 'inspired and sustained not only Catholic beliefs but also Lithuanian nationality.'[16] The national movement intensified, with demands by 1905 for Lithuanian autonomy or independence. The opportunity was realised in the course of World War I[17] with the destruction of the Tsarist regime and the achievement of Lithuanian autonomy. On 16 February 1918, the Council of Lithuania proclaimed Lithuanian independence, with the Soviet Union one of the first nations to recognise Lithuania *de jure*. Lithuania's second largest city Kaunas remained the provisional capital for the next two decades, during which time the national economy, destroyed by World War I, was rebuilt on the basis of land reform and industrial and agricultural development.[18]

During the years of independence Lithuania became a full member of the world community and followed a policy of non-alignment. It created its own system of education, including education of ethnic minorities, and reinstated Lithuanian as the official language in schools. Compulsory primary education of four (later six) years was introduced and a Lithuanian University opened in Kaunas.[19] The advances in education played an important role in laying the groundwork for national consciousness among Lithuanian youth. The poetry of prominent Lithuanian writers drawing from folklore and songs was celebrated. In 1924 National Song Festivals were initiated, with 77 choirs and a total of 3,000 singers taking part. Lithuania became a regular participant in the Olympic Games. The revitalisation of cultural and sporting traditions gained international recognition for Lithuania, consolidating the sense of national and cultural identity that accompanied the country's economic and social growth. But, as in the past, the danger of occupation by neighbouring states was ever present.[20]

## German–Russian war and the aftermath 1939–1944

On 23 August 1939, the Soviet Union and Germany signed the Molotov–Ribbentrop Pact, with its secret protocol for carving up Eastern Europe. The Pact enabled the German partition of Poland and the transfer of the Baltic states to the Soviet Union. On 14 June 1940, the Soviets occupied the three

Baltic states and formed transitional 'People's Governments'. The following month, local communists faithful to Moscow rigged parliamentary elections for the 'People's Parliaments'. The Lithuanian constitution was ignored and Soviet rule imposed. The Lithuanian President was forced to leave the country. Incorporation into the Soviet Union was followed by rigged elections, with local candidates selected into the Parliament against their will. With the People's Parliament surrounded by the secret police, the new government legalised the Lithuanian Communist Party (CPL). At the time of the Soviet invasion, Party membership was negligible – just 0.06 per cent of the three million population. It increased in later years but, tellingly, in 1949, half of the members of the CPL Central Committee were non-Lithuanians, and the CPL was considered one of the weakest Communist Parties of the Soviet Republics.[21]

Religious activities were suppressed. On 1 July 1940, the relationship with the Vatican was ended and three of the four seminaries in Lithuania closed. Kaunas Seminary, tolerated at first, was turned into Red Army quarters. The religious press was closed, and religious books destroyed. Soviets took charge of church rectories, cutting off clergy salaries. The Soviet 'friendship', Lithuanians were assured, was to protect them from Nazi aggression.[22]

The greatest impact of Soviet totalitarianism was felt in agriculture, with the collectivisation of Lithuanian farms. On 22 July 1940, even before Lithuania was incorporated into the Soviet Union, the People's Parliament declared all privately owned land state property. The establishment of *kolkhoses* (collective farms) and *sovkhoses* (state farms) devastated the successful 'small-scale' cooperative farming practices established during the years of Lithuanian independence. Agriculture became dysfunctional to the point that the Lithuanian government had to appeal to Moscow for bread.[23]

On 3 August 1940, Moscow admitted Lithuania into the Soviet Union and executed the act of annexation. Exactly three weeks later, the People's Parliament became the Supreme Soviet of the Lithuanian Soviet Socialist Republic, its new constitution – a copy of the other Soviet Republics – proclaiming 'Stalin's genius'.[24]

Soviet occupation was met with resistance from students, workers, farmers and the intelligentsia. People boycotted elections to the People's Parliament, and refused to observe the introduced Soviet holidays of 7 November and 1 May. In September 1940, handwritten anti-Soviet leaflets were systematically distributed in educational institutions and on the streets with the following slogans: 'Long live independent Lithuania', 'Lithuania for the Lithuanians', and 'Down with the communist terror'. Underground activities continued in the cities of Vilnius and Kaunas, as well as in 15 counties. People from all levels of society were united in their determination to reinstate Lithuanian independence, with high school and university students, peasants and professionals coming together in groups such as the Independent Party, the Committee for Liberation of Lithuania, and the Committee to Help Lithuania.[25]

On 25 November 1940, a decree incorporating the Lithuanian economy into that of the USSR was passed and the Soviet ruble became the official currency. Soon the country was 'Sovietised' in all fields. The brutality of Stalinism spread fear, hatred, tension and distrust among the people. So-called 'national problems', or claims of statehood, were simply 'solved' by deportation. Those deported were the best educated, and their loss greatly weakened the economic, social and cultural capital of the nation. The decision was taken to deport one-third of the Lithuanian population – the so-called 'anti-Soviet elements' – by the end of May 1941. The mass deportations began at 4 am on 14 June 1941; people were given 15 minutes to pack and entire families were taken to railway depots for departure in cattle wagons. Documentation of these instructions discovered after the Soviet retreat show that 531 cattle wagons were registered in Naujoji Vilnia near Vilnius as having human cargo, while 340 cattle wagons took other routes. The number of people placed in one wagon was supposed to be 25, but in reality the number exceeded 50 persons per cattle wagon. It has been estimated that 34,260 Lithuanians were deported in a span of a few days, the records of the People's Commissariat for Internal Affairs – in which Russians occupied three quarters of the leading positions – showing that deportees were sent to Siberia, North Russia, Karelia or Kazakhstan.[26]

The second mass deportation, scheduled for 24 June 1941, was disrupted by the German–Russian war. By then people were acutely aware that the Stalinist regime entailed suffering and uncertainty at both the individual and national levels. Although nationalistic sentiment was silenced, the underground resistance persisted, with widespread popular mistrust towards Soviet sympathisers.[27]

With the nationalisation of business enterprises, peasants lost their land and farmers were financially ruined by discriminatory requisition of agricultural products. Factory workers suffered from the increased cost of living and the disappearance of goods available in stores. All the while, opponents of the Soviet regime were incarcerated in the prisons of Lithuania and Russia. Members of the clergy and religious adherents were persecuted. But more than any other factor, it was the mass deportation of civilians that ignited anti-Soviet hatred across the country. In the circumstances, it is understandable that many Lithuanians awaited the arrival of Nazi Germans with the hope that things would improve,[28] though for people like myself who had grown up in the postwar Soviet system it was inconceivable to imagine any justification for pro-German sentiment. That awareness only came after I left Lithuania and was exposed, for the first time, to the perspectives of Lithuanians opposed to Soviet rule.

From the perspective of many of the postwar refugees who settled in Australia, there was a collective sigh of relief when, on 22 June 1941, Nazi Germany began its war against the Soviet Union and entered Lithuania. On 8 August, the Reichskommissariat Ostland issued a decree declaring Germany the legal heir to the Soviet Union. The decree gave power to the Ostland German civilian administration to take over all the Soviet-nationalised property, land, realty, industry and commerce. The Nazis accepted Soviet nationalisation because it meant that they could 'inherit' nationalised property: *kolkhoses* and *sovkhoses* were retained and the owners of the land remained as the hired workers of the Nazis.[29] The Provisional Lithuanian government formed just before the Germans arrived soon discovered that the Nazis did not intend to share power. 'Persuaded' that a small nation like Lithuania could not be independent, after just six weeks of existence, the provisional government had to declare itself 'involuntarily suspended'. Lithuanians, who had naively greeted the advancing Germans as 'true liberators', were left feeling vulnerable and mistrusting. It soon became apparent that the Germans planned to colonise Lithuania, using twin policies of Germanisation and deportation to destroy the native population.[30]

A conference was organised in May 1943 to try to ease tensions between Germany and Lithuania and counter communist partisans in the eastern region 'supported and supplied from the Soviet Union'.[31] In February 1944, it was agreed that a local Lithuanian troop detachment (Litauische streikrafte) consisting of volunteers would be formed under the guidance of General Povilas Plechavičius. The Germans were surprised with the success of recruitment, with Lithuanian commands limiting their role to the territory of Lithuanian proper, but the Germans had other ideas.[32] In May 1944 Plechavičius and other members of staff were arrested and deported to concentration camp in Salaspilis, Latvia. The Lithuanian detachment was liquidated by executions and random shootings, and the further arrest of 3,500 people. Resistors were forced into labour camps in Germany. Others joined the armed Lithuanian underground, formed 'to fight the second Soviet occupation of Lithuania.'[33] The determination of Lithuanians to hold onto their separate identity was attested to by Stasys Raštikis, former Lithuanian commander in chief:

> Larger nations than Lithuania were not able to withstand the Nazi German pressures. They had to provide the Germans with national SS legions, divisions, brigades, and other SS units. The French, Danes, Norwegians, Spaniards, Horvatians, Albanians, Slovaks, Romanians, Hungarians, Russians, Ukrainians, Byelorussians, Estonians, Latvians, and others had formed such units. The Lithuanians and the Poles were the only East Europeans who did not provide the Germans with an SS unit.[34]

During the German occupation some 20,000 Lithuanians who had been forced to fight with the Red army surrendered *en masse* to the German occupiers. Most were accepted into German-led units. Some 75,000 Lithuanians were taken to Germany for compulsory labour duties. Rebels were sent to concentration camps. The German invasion of Lithuania greatly affected the Lithuanian sense of national belonging, with some nationals taking advantage of the German presence by 'adopting' a German identity and others sympathising with the Nazis. But overall, according to historian Andres Kasekamp, Germanisation in the Baltic region did not materialise.[35]

## *1940s 'cleansing' campaign*

When the Red army was again marching towards Lithuanian territory in June 1944, memories of the mass deportations to Siberia were still fresh in people's minds. The Soviet army took Vilnius on 13 July and reoccupied Lithuania. A partisan resistance force engaged in a guerrilla campaign across Lithuania for the next eight years, during which time Stalin resumed his 'cleansing' campaign, targeting the political, religious and intellectual elite. Many Lithuanian leaders were killed or sent into exile, and during a six-year period some 350,000 people were deported.[36]

When the Soviets introduced radical land reform in August 1944, people fled their homes. With the German defeat in the Baltic territories the following month, approximately 60,000–100,000 Lithuanians sought refuge in Germany.[37] It has been estimated that in 1945 the number of Lithuanian refugees in Displaced Persons (DP) camps in all of Western Europe was 63,000. The rest of those that fled Lithuania lived outside the DP camps, or were killed or otherwise perished. Those who fled – townspeople, rich farmers, members of the intelligentsia and army officers – thought it was only a temporary departure and anticipated that they would soon return home. Though impoverished and devastated, Nazi Germany was regarded as 'the only available escape route.'[38] Germans and Lithuanians used the same escape route, the panic and chaos of the retreating German army extending to the Lithuanian refugees, who travelled in carriages and on foot. Nobody controlled the borders as people jumped on trains or walked for days from one German town to the next.[39]

Until DP camps were organised, Lithuanians who fled to war-devastated Germany lived among ruins. Some were sheltered by the locals. Germany surrendered on 8 May 1945, and following the Potsdam Conference was divided by the Allies into four Occupation Zones. Some refugees spent four years or more in DP camps before migrating to the United States, Canada, Venezuela, Argentina and Australia. During their stay in the camps, some Lithuanians experienced unfriendly German attitudes and hopeless prospects, which encouraged them to emigrate.[40] Others experienced local generosity, one recalling how 'German women were waiting to feed refugees at every train stop. Although locals were also starving, they fed us soup, sausages and bread.' Another recalls how German farmers received Lithuanians well and 'did not want them to leave.'[41] My own maternal grandmother and her four daughters lived with a German family from 1944 to 1948 and were encouraged to stay on and help on the farm. The future was less rosy for Lithuanians who settled in the DP camps, where they were encouraged by Soviet authorities to return home. They felt a danger to their lives and were afraid of being forced to go back to Soviet Lithuania. They regarded themselves as exiles from the 'Lithuanian nation'. Their comradeship with each other and their efforts to maintain their national and cultural activities reinforced their collective identity. Those who had relatives who had settled in the United States before World War I wanted to join them. However, American quotas 'were tight', whereas Australia was suffering a labour shortage, and the 9,906 Lithuanians who settled in Australia between 1947 and 1953 were some 6 per cent of the total of 170,000 DPs who arrived during this period. But the feeling of being exiles never left the postwar Australian Lithuanian generation. While they had escaped the grip of Soviet communism, in Australia they found 24,000 card-carrying communists, many of them influential in trade unions, media, universities and even churches. To recount stories of Soviet brutality and mass deportations raised suspicions among many Australians, who felt grateful to Soviet Russia for having sacrificed 20–27 million lives defeating Nazi Germany.[42]

The sense of exilic isolation was reinforced by government actions, such as the Liberal–Country Party government signing a trade mission with

Russia in 1965, and the Labor government's recognition of Soviet sovereignty over the Baltic states in 1974. Politicians promoted the 'advantages' of the arrangement, such as settlement of estates and family reunion, but those familiar with the Soviet system were unconvinced. For the next 17 months they campaigned to reverse the government decision, and *de jure* recognition was finally downgraded to *de facto* recognition in December 1975. This still left Baltic people feeling vulnerable about their relationship with their homeland and its people had been influenced by continuing Soviet propaganda to view the Soviet citizens who did not return to their homelands after the war as 'traitors of the state'.[43]

## *Split of the Lithuanian nation*

Those who remained in Lithuania after the war experienced further threats of deportation under the tightening Soviet grip. The people deported for political reasons were replaced by Russians, Ukrainians and Byelorussians. As postwar industrialisation intensified, many left the countryside for the city. This was a further challenge to prewar Lithuanian identity, but with more Lithuanians going to university to acquire the skills necessary for the workplace, there were few vacancies for Russians. Intermarriage posed another challenge, but as children from mixed marriages generally identified with the Lithuanian parent it did not result in any pronounced Russification. Ethnic homogeneity persisted.

Lithuanian homogeneity was tolerated because of the country's compliance with Moscow's control. The Lithuanian ruling party under Antanas Sniečkus had been given certain privileges, with Stalin reportedly quipping that he and Sniečkus 'were the only real communists left in the whole of the Soviet Union.'[44] But while the Lithuanian leader carried out Moscow's order to deport Lithuanians with 'great enthusiasm', he balanced his strong Lithuanian nationalist sentiments by 'sabotaging some orders of Moscow, [and] demanding some privileges for Lithuania …'[45] Overall, Sniečkus maintained his 'good relationship' with Moscow by subjecting Lithuanians who had not emigrated to the policies of the Soviet Communist

Party, which sought to control the lives and thoughts of all Soviet citizens. From the perspective of the Communist Party – which was also Sniečkus's perspective – the aim was to build a classless society

> with one form of public ownership of the means of production and full social equality of all members of society; under it, the all-round development of people will be accompanied by the growth of the productive forces through continuous progress in science and technology; all the springs of cooperative wealth will flow more abundantly, and the great principle 'From each according to his ability, to each according to his needs' will be implemented. Communism is a highly organised society of free, socially conscious working people in which public self-government will be established, a society in which labour for the good of society will become the prime vital requirement of everyone, a necessity recognised by one and all, and the ability of each person will be employed to the greatest benefit of the people.[46]

Mirroring this idealistic vision at the national level, it was assumed that under communism nations would 'draw closer and closer together in all spheres on the basis of a complete identity of economic, political, and spiritual interests of fraternal friendship and cooperation.'[47]

Theoretically, nationalistic feelings would become irrelevant given the brotherhood of communist society – though in fact the Soviet communism utopia was closely related to the process of Russification, with 'non-Russians … transformed objectively and psychologically into Russians.'[48] Non-Russian national feelings were suppressed and the voices of the other Soviet Union nations silenced. While later Soviet leaders Nikita Khrushchev and Leonid Brezhnev tolerated non-Russian nationalism by allowing Soviet Republics to publish in their native tongues and culturally express themselves in plays, films and books, when non-Russian nationalities became 'too enthusiastic in celebrating national achievements, they were silenced.'[49]

As Soviet citizens, Lithuanians like myself were constantly exposed to the terms 'internationalism', 'Soviet patriotism' or 'the Soviet people'. At the same time, the 'superiority' of the Russian people was emphasised. Lithuania's national culture was suppressed and the nation's past 'deemphasised' by the state. The spread of a Russian worldview and consciousness was not particularly creative – with traffic signals, advertisements and inscriptions presented in both Lithuanian and Russian, and some agencies' documents written in Russian only – but was nonetheless effective, with Lithuanian writers and philologists expressing concern about the weakening of the Lithuanian language among intellectuals. All doctoral dissertations had to be written in Russian, and Russian radio and television broadcasting, together with Russian books, were heavily promoted with the gradual implementation of 'virtual bilingualism'.[50] Implicitly, the Soviet ideological apparatus was designed to encourage Russification.

Despite the evidence that it could 'neither give them freedom nor provide them with bread', there were Lithuanian intellectuals who sincerely believed in communism and Marxism-Leninism.[51] Reflecting back now, it is clear that this was the direct outcome of Soviet education, which denied people the information that would have enabled them to challenge the dogma to which we were constantly exposed in school, through the media and at work. In the school curriculum, Lithuanian history was caricatured and distorted, at the same time as the Russian curriculum was intensified. Starting with linguistic blending, the process was designed to gradually merge people's separate national and cultural identities into a unified Soviet identity. To assimilate all Soviet citizens into the one Russified identity, non-Russians, like Lithuanians, were expected to detach themselves from their own national and cultural identities. Ostensibly the model was neutral, but we knew full well that the words 'Centre' and 'Soviet' meant 'Russia' and 'Russian hegemony'. Officially we were encouraged to celebrate our national achievements, but these achievements were diluted and robbed of their meaning-making power by the Russianised national and cultural elements – and there was the ever-present sense that non-Russian nationalities were closely observed by Soviet apparatchiks.[52]

## 1970s–1980s

Faced with intensified national movements among non-Russian nationalities in the 1970s, the Soviet ruling apparatus strengthened its powers. The role of the KGB was upgraded. Intellectuals were under special suspicion. Dean of the Linguistics Faculty at Kapsukas University and internationally-known specialist in Baltic linguistics Professor Jonas Kazlauskas mysteriously disappeared on a Vilnius street in October 1970 and was found floating in the river Neris. The newspaper *Tiesa* (Truth) did not carry an obituary, nor did the University or party representatives offer the customary eulogy at his funeral. It is generally accepted that the 40-year-old scholar had a conflict with the authorities, and most likely with the KGB which appears to have mishandled the case.[53]

In November 1970, radio operator Simas Kudirka from the ship *Sovetskaya Litva* (Soviet Lithuania) tried to defect to the United States by jumping overboard. Although he successfully reached the Coast Guard cutter *Vigilant* moored alongside the Soviet ship at Martha's Vineyard Massachusetts, the Soviets were allowed to board the cutter and forcibly seize the defector and return him to the *Sovetskaya Litva,* where he was badly beaten before being returned to Lithuania to be put on trial as an illegal defector. Sentenced to ten years in a strict regime camp, Kudirka pleaded his innocence on the basis of the Universal Declaration of Human Rights and the Soviet constitution. America eventually prevailed upon the Soviets to release Kudirka on the grounds that his mother was born in the United States and that they both were US citizens.[54]

Kudirka's stand expressed the thoughts of many at a time when the Soviets were faced with a newly reborn anti-communist nationalism. Non-conformist youth conceived the idea of making the Lithuanian struggle for freedom known to the world. Although Lithuanian youth had learned 'to live and work like Lenin', the Komsomol (Young Communist League) of Soviet Lithuania was 'plagued by problems'[55], and occasionally the entire leadership of the organisation had to be removed. So even among Komsomols, nationalistic feelings remained strong. In terms of religion, many young people chose to become agnostic but not atheist. Their anti-Soviet sentiment was fed by the youth 'revolution' in the West, with Western youth supporting leftist revolutionary demands. In 1971–72, the most popular music in private gatherings was the music of the independent Lithuanian period, competing with the American musical *Jesus Christ Superstar*, which captured Lithuanian youth's spirit of protest and their search for personal freedom that was not accessible behind the 'iron curtain'.[56]

In May 1972, a group of young Lithuanian rebels took advantage of US President Nixon's visit to Moscow to make a stand. On 14 May, in the park of the Musical Theatre in the centre of Kaunas, 19-year-old Lithuanian Romas Kalanta took off his shirt, poured liquid over his body, and turned himself into a living torch. 'I am dying for the freedom of Lithuania' were his last words.[57] In order to avoid a 'chain reaction', police tightened their patrols in Kaunas. Masses of young people gathered in front of Kalanta's home, disregarding a government spokesman's instruction for them to go home. Applauding their own speakers and denouncing Moscow's rule over Lithuania, the crowd moved through Laisvės alėja (Freedom Boulevard) with placards carrying the messages 'Freedom for Lithuania' and 'We are not against socialism but for a free Lithuania'. Other slogans demanded freedom of religion. Five days later special security forces arrested about 500 people. There were at least three more attempts at self-immolation to protest against Soviet rule, in the towns of Kaunas and Kapsukas (now Marijampolė). Party secretary Antanas Sniečkus put the massive support for Kalanta down to 'bourgeois ideology' and its attempt 'to poison the consciousness of the working people with the poison of nationalism.'[58] The fear of being persecuted by the authorities was strong, but non-conformist Lithuanian youth showed the world that Soviet power to curtail nationalist movements within the USSR was waning. The more authorities tried to suppress their opposition, the more the people of Lithuania rose up against the totalitarian regime.

In 1972, the underground publication *The chronicle of the Catholic Church in Lithuania* presented disturbing facts of religious persecution which violated not only the Soviet and the Lithuanian constitutions, but also the Universal Declaration of Human Rights. 'Children were scolded by their teachers for attending mass and told that if they persisted they would not get into the university.'[59] Their parents risked losing their jobs if they persisted with Catholic beliefs, and faced long jail terms for 'anti-Soviet' behaviour. But Catholic resistance remained strong, as documented in the *samizdat* (self-published) *chronicles* and the testimony of Lithuanians 'who fled or were expelled from the Soviet Union for their anti-Soviet activities.'[60] In many respects, religion served as a proxy for Lithuanian nationalism, which had survived despite the Soviet campaign to destroy it.

During the 1970s, Brezhnev's leadership continued to struggle against 'bourgeois ideology' and 'outside interference' in Soviet affairs. The harsh treatment of dissidents by the Soviet authorities became an issue in relations with Western democracies. The Soviet signing of the Final Act of the Conference on Security and Cooperation in Europe (CSCE) in 1975 constituted an important step towards the linkage of arms control and East-West trade with Soviet human rights. Soviet dissidents increasingly appealed to the United Nations and Western agencies, including human rights organisations Amnesty International and Helsinki Watch. The smuggling of privately circulated *samizdat* writings abroad and the transmission of their content back into the USSR via Western radio broadcasts ensured that information about national dissidents reached large numbers of Soviet citizens.[61]

Dissidents still faced the coercive power of the Soviet state. After spending 25 years in prison for 'dangerous offences against the state',[62] former non-communist party member Balys Gajauskas was finally released in 1973 after serving his full sentence. In 1978 the Supreme Court of the Lithuanian SSR examined a new case against Gajauskas, claiming that since his release he had spread anti-Soviet propaganda in order to undermine and weaken the Soviet government. Gajauskas was accused of keeping anti-Soviet literature and circulating it to people with similar views – for example, disseminating volume one of Alexander Solzhenitsyn's *The Gulag Archipelago*, which Gajauskas apparently had translated into Lithuanian. He pleaded not guilty, but was sentenced to ten years in prison and five years in exile.[63] Growing up in Lithuania during this period, I was hardly aware of resistance to Soviet control, as the authorities made every effort to suppress such information circulating among the population.

Information about prominent citizens who emigrated overseas was also suppressed. The Lithuanian intellectual Tomas Venclova, who translated into Lithuanian many well-known works of Western literature such as James Joyce's *Ulysses,* displayed non-conformist attitudes towards the Soviet system. In 1975 he asked the Central Committee of the Lithuanian Communist Party for permission to emigrate on the grounds that he had limited 'public literary, scientific, and cultural' opportunities. Venclova was allowed to leave with a visa for five years, but two years later he was stripped of his citizenship 'for behaviour smearing the name of a Soviet citizen.'[64]

Try as it might to suppress 'potentially subversive' personal opinion, in practice the regime was unable to stop people privately airing their views about the Soviet system through jokes and anecdotes. All around us we could see for ourselves that the Soviet Union in itself was corrupt and corrupting, encouraging people to enjoy the benefits of the failing communism utopia, teaching its citizens to use the system to their own advantage, and encouraging laziness and mistrust. Even those of us who were not hostile to communism could not help but see how Soviet rule was transforming the 'enthusiastic worker' into a completely (in)different Soviet citizen: deeply dissatisfied and drowning his sorrows in drugs and alcohol. Constant shortages of material goods and the difficulty of leading the uncorrupt life led to an obsession with trying to buy a dwelling, a car or clothes.[65]

Many felt the absurdity of the Soviet system and viewed the Communist Party as a perfect example of a corrupt society. By 1984 membership of the Communist Lithuanian Party had reached 5.25 per cent compared with 6.75 per cent in the Communist Party of the Soviet Union. Many Lithuanians had joined the CPL to comply with Moscow's pressure. Only a few Lithuanian intellectuals did not join. Some Lithuanians joined the Party in order to acquire privileges associated with membership, at the same time rejecting the designation 'Soviet' and retaining a strong sense of being Lithuanian. The irony is that membership of the CPL brought with it greater appreciation of the corruption of the Soviet system. Algimantas Čekuolis, a former Soviet apparatchik, knew from the inside that the system was a 'giant pool of shit':

> Anyone who achieved any prominence in this society knew that the Soviet system was rotten and corrupt. In my travels throughout the USSR, I always carried two suitcases – one with my clothes and personal things, and a second with gifts for the party leaders I intended to meet. The bigger the official, the bigger the gift. Surprisingly, it was the little people who kept believing in the system long after the rest of us knew that it was a giant pool of shit![66]

Algirdas Degutis, later a libertarian who argued that government has no right to interfere 'in private affairs under any circumstances', acknowledged that he had been a true believer in Marxism-Leninism. He recalls even trying to convince his father that it was a good thing they had been deported to Siberia, because 'driving Lithuanians from their homeland would destroy bourgeois society and set the stage for building a new, Soviet society in its place.'[67] Degutis came from a family of *kulaks* (farmers), who were considered a threat to the Soviets, despite no involvement in politics. Outwardly people may have 'remained faithful' to the totalitarian regime, but with the introduction of Gorbachev's policy of *glasnost* after 1985 hidden and inchoate nationalistic feelings began to surface. When Gorbachev suddenly relaxed the system of political repression, national movements in the Soviet Union emerged as a mass-organised political force, challenging Soviet rule. The years 1986 to 1988 were regarded as a period of national reawakening, with the Baltic people exposed for the first time during Soviet rule to a public rediscovery of their history. Suppressed feelings resurfaced and there was open organised opposition to the incorporation of the Baltic states into the Soviet Union, as well as calls for human rights and religious freedom. It was a reawakening of national consciousness, replete with pre-Soviet national symbols. As in other parts of the Soviet Union, *glasnost* spawned a plethora of grassroots-based social movements across the Soviet nations, calling for greater economic, political and cultural autonomy.[68]

### *Regaining independence: 1990s*

By 1990 a growing number of Lithuanian intellectuals were challenging the Soviet version of Lithuanian history. Resentment against the unjust regime, previously expressed in the safety and privacy of a friend's kitchen, was expressed publicly in mass gatherings across the nation, culminating in Lithuania's secession from the Soviet Union. During the All Soviet elections for the Supreme Soviet in February 1990, free elections took place in Vilnius – the first in the history of the Soviet 'empire'. On 11 March, the Supreme Soviet of the Lithuanian SSR elected the Lithuanian Supreme Council, which proclaimed Lithuanian independence – the first Soviet Republic to do so in the 72 years of the Soviet Union. Gorbachev denounced the declaration of independence as unconstitutional and imposed an economic blockade on Lithuania. The denunciations were counter-productive, the people closing ranks around their democratically elected leaders. Neither the Kremlin nor the Lithuanian people were prepared to back down. Gorbachev admitted that 'we underestimated the forces of nationalism and separatism that were hidden deep within our system ... creating a socially explosive mixture.'[69]

On 1 January 1991, Soviet troops seized the Lithuanian Communist Party headquarters, and on 11 January the Vilnius Press Centre came under Soviet control. Two days later, Soviet tanks surrounded the Vilnius Radio and Television Broadcasting Centre and the Television Tower, protected by some 1,000 unarmed people singing Lithuanian national songs. The tanks were driven into the crowds and over the people, killing 14 and injuring close to 300. The event only strengthened nationalistic outrage, Vytautas Landsbergis, the first freely-elected President of Lithuania, explaining the self-sacrifice by declaring: 'people do not lie in front of tanks and risk their lives for better kitchen appliances.'[70]

Underestimated forces of nationalism and separatism that were hidden deep within the Soviet system resulted in Moscow's political power struggle. The 19–21 August 1991 putsch by a group of the government representatives destabilised Gorbachev's leadership and further weakened Soviet control, and had the effect of further strengthening national solidarity among the Baltic states. On 6 September 1991, the newly formed State Council of the USSR formally accepted that Estonia, Latvia and Lithuania were no longer part of the USSR.[71]

Formal independence did not solve the historic, political and socio-economic problems created during 50 years of Soviet rule. As early as 1992, nationalist sentiment was in danger of being swamped by the problems of economic instability: jobs, wages, pensions, security and the cost of living in an underdeveloped free-market. President Landsbergis aimed to 'shed the culture of Homo Sovieticus' (Soviet Man) and restore Lithuania to its 'pre-Soviet status' of independence and growing prosperity between the two World Wars. He believed that the restoration of Lithuania would. But with Russia retaining control of gas and oil and without the expertise to build a capitalist economy in the existing political environment, it was impossible for Lithuania to break away completely from its neighbor. Lithuania, like all other post-Soviet nations, had to begin the process of independent existence from scratch.[72]

Idealistic expectations were dashed. Former members of the Communist Party exploited political contacts to accumulate personal wealth. Political corruption was widespread. By bribing officials, it was possible to purchase private property or engage in commercial enterprise. Intellectuals, who had held prestigious positions and been rewarded by high wages in the past, had their salaries slashed. In order to make ends meet, many worked two jobs, while others found themselves out of work. Economic deprivation led to a growing desire to look for opportunities abroad, something that had been denied to young people aspiring to a more affluent or autonomous life under Soviet rule.[73] By 2000, 51 per cent of Lithuania's youth felt pessimistic about the future and 72 per cent were contemplating going overseas for temporary work or emigrating permanently. A survey two years later found that between 120,000 and 130,000 people had emigrated from Lithuania during the previous 12 years, and that nearly 79 per cent of Lithuanians aged 29 and under wanted to leave the country temporarily or permanently. In 2003, the Lithuanian General Consul in Chicago wrote that since independence approximately one million Lithuanians had moved away from the homeland, with some 30,000 settling in Chicago alone. Six and a half thousand had won 'the green card', allowing them to live and work in the US, and three out of five of those who initially gained their visa from the US Embassy in Lithuania remained in the country illegally after its expiry date. According to the Lithuanian Bureau of Statistics, 54,300 people left Lithuania in 2011, mostly for the United Kingdom, Ireland and Germany. Nearly half were between 20 and 29 years of age. The Lithuanian population of 3.717 million in 1995 shrank to 3.2 million in 2011.[74] Despite independence and the ability to reclaim national and cultural identity, what the figures show is that many Lithuanians were prepared to exchange their nationalistic sentiments for better opportunities abroad.

The values and attitudes they carried abroad differed from those of the postwar refugees. But throughout its long history, Lithuania's national and cultural identity has continually evolved and changed. Pagan religion and the emergence of a distinctive language had initially played a vital part in shaping Lithuanian identity. Then, under the influence of neighbouring countries, religious identity changed, though Lithuanian clergy and intellectuals encouraged rural Lithuanian folk to retain their language and traditions in order to immunise themselves against the influence of Poles and other Slavs. Resistance to Polonisation and Russification was rewarded after World War I, when Lithuania gained its independence, and for the next 22 years economic and social development nourished a strong sense of national and cultural revival. Independence was lost during World War II, first to the Soviets and then to the Germans. The defeat of the Nazis saw tens of thousands of Lithuanians fleeing their homeland for refuge abroad, where they nurtured the cultural rebirth they had experienced during the independent interregnum. Those who chose, or were forced, to stay and live under the Soviet order acquired a different sense of self and of culture. In the 1980s, strong nationalistic feelings resurfaced, and with Lithuania regaining its independence in 1991, Lithuanians had to learn again how to live as an independent nation – a process that continues.

Depending on when and under what circumstances they left Lithuania, refugees and emigrants carried with them different experiences and understandings of national and cultural identity. The 60,000–100,000 who fled abroad after the defeat of the Germans and the reimposition of Soviet rule held onto memories of forced collectivisation and deportation, with their land confiscated and relatives and friends killed or exiled to Siberia – and the history of Soviet control right up to the 1990s only served to confirm their negative memories. In Europe's DP camps they cemented a strong collective identity of what it meant to be Lithuanian, and – as we shall see in the following chapter – many of the 10,000 who arrived in Australia after 1947 were determined to preserve at all costs their unique Lithuanian identity, safe from Soviet and, indeed, Australian influence.

CHAPTER 2

# Constructing 'Lithuania' in Australia: post-World War II Lithuanian refugees

## *Resettlement*

At the Yalta Conference in February 1945, the British and American Allies agreed to repatriate 'liberated prisoners of war and civilians'[1] from each other's countries. The United Nations Relief and Rehabilitation Administration (UNRRA) was charged with speeding up the refugee repatriation, and between May and September 1945 many of the Displaced Persons or DPs who had fled from the Soviet Union were forced to return to their home countries. People who had survived Nazi captivity attracted Soviet suspicion and their repatriation was brutal. The Soviet government argued that DPs were Soviet citizens and 'without the government's permission, no individual renunciation of citizenship is valid.'[2] While the Allied leaders agreed that 'all Soviet citizens' must be repatriated 'from enemy territory', there was confusion between who should be regarded as Soviet citizens and 'claimants to Soviet nationality'.[3] Reinterpreting their earlier agreement with the USSR, the British and American authorities repatriated only those who claimed Soviet citizenship.[4] Uncertain of their future, people from the Soviet Union were afraid to return home. There was unrest and suicides in the American and British territories. Some Soviet troops escaped by jumping overboard or they killed themselves before their forced return. Upon their return to the Soviet Union, 1.8 million military personnel and 3.6 million civilians were thoroughly checked through special Narodny Komissariat Vnutrennih Del (People's Commissariat of Internal Affairs) or NKVD filtration camps. For some the process took years. Others received long prison terms. Others were shot straight away.[5]

Pressure from the International Refugee Organisation (IRO) for countries to revise their immigration restrictions towards DPs succeeded in the case of Canada and Australia, but not the United States, where Congress was reluctant to accept Jews and Eastern Europeans. However, in 1948 an agreement to absorb 200,000 DPs was signed and by 1952 22,771 Lithuanian, 34,800 Latvian and 9,811 Estonian refugees were admitted to the US. For its part, the IRO conducted regular screenings 'in order to find possible war criminals and Nazis, as well as Soviet citizens and others who were not entitled to the IRO's aid.'[6]

All Baltic people were regarded as Soviet citizens because the Baltic states had been incorporated into the Soviet Union, where refugees were referred to as 'Nazis', 'Fascists', 'undemocratic', 'criminal', 'undesirable elements', 'diversionists', 'spies', 'saboteurs' and 'traitors.' As war crimes historian Ruth Betinna Birn has noted, the term collaborator, implying traitor, was inaccurately used against those that collaborated with the Nazis, 'since the state to whom they owed allegiance had already been destroyed by the USSR.'[7] Caught between German and Russian war politics, Lithuanians, Latvians and Estonians 'had little opportunity to make morally untainted choices between two evils.'[8] The primary motive among Baltic DPs for refusing to return was, as Jonathan H. L'Hommedieu has documented, political fear.[9] The issue galvanised the Baltic DP community. Lithuanians, like others, regarded themselves as political refugees who did not want to return to Soviet-occupied Lithuania. In accord with 1947 IRO procedures, under the UNRRA all refugees became stateless and their passports invalid. The solution came as countries such as Belgium, Great Britain, Canada, Australia, and later Venezuela, French Morocco, Argentina, Brazil and France, began to accept refugees.[10]

## *From stateless refugees to new Australians*

Australia's commitment to take DPs in the post-World War II period altered the ethnic balance of the population. As James Jupp has noted, at the end of the war Australia was considered 'too thinly populated and too reliant on primary industry.'[11] The choice for the largely monocultural country was 'populate or perish', and the Chifley postwar Labor government decided to accept mass migration from war-torn Europe, including the preferred source country Britain. With around 1.6 million people in Europe displaced as a result of the war, Australia signed an agreement with the Preparatory Commission for the International Refugee Organisation (PCIRO) to accept an annual quota of 12,000 DPs. They were recruited from the DP camps of Central Europe, and Australia's first Minister for Immigration, Arthur Calwell, personally visited the camps and was impressed with the blue-eyed, blond-haired, fair-skinned 'Balts' – Lithuanians, Latvians and Estonians – who fitted the 'good type' category. Calwell's successor Harold Holt, Minister for Immigration in the conservative Menzies government from 1949–66, considered Balts 'particularly important' for Australia's postwar immigration program, as 'their capacity to fit into the Australian pattern would influence the Australian attitude to migration as a whole …'[12]

As refugees, DPs agreed to conditions which James Jupp considers 'would have been rejected by voluntarily migrants.' They were shipped to Australia by troop carriers and housed in former army camps. Bound by a two-year work contract, refugees were eligible only for work as 'labourers' and 'domestics', mirroring 'the terms used for so many assisted British migrants in the previous century.'[13]

More than 80 per cent of the Lithuanians had lived in DP camps in Western Germany for four or more years before coming to Australia. According to my own research among Lithuanian community activists,[14] decades after settling in Australia the overwhelming majority of postwar refugees still described their nationality as Lithuanian – rather than Australian or naturalised Australian, or Lithuanian Australian or Australian Lithuanian. There were some who called themselves distinctly Lithuanian or definitely Australian.[15] Others remarked that they had taken on more than one national identity. One respondent admitted to feeling 70 per cent Lithuanian and considered that he would never be Australian. Another was puzzled: 'People ask me that question and it is very hard. I came to Australia as Lithuanian. My passport says I am Australian. I guess I am 50-50.' Other responses included: identifying as Lithuanian in Australia but as Australian when travelling overseas, and difficulty distinguishing between the two national identities.

What the responses indicate is that terms such as 'citizenship', 'nationality' and 'ethnicity' have diverse meanings, and can change meaning in different contexts. Australian Latvian researcher Aldis L Putniņš distinguishes between citizenship – 'a political concept denoting formal allegiance to a particular state' – and nationality, which 'originates from the political concept of a nation and denotes membership of a nation state.' Given that nationality is 'often used as a synonym for ethnicity' whereas ethnicity is not synonymous with either race or nationality,[16] the respondents' confusion is understandable.

It has been estimated that during the Soviet era, of the 0.75 to 1.25 million Australians holding dual citizenship, 0.5 million were dual Australian/Soviet citizens. According to Algimantas Taškūnas, 'Nearly all naturalised Australians of Baltic origin belong to this category.'[17] The 1971 Australian Census indicates that between 1945 and 1966, out of a total of 36,613 Baltic migrants, 33,545 became Australian citizens, at which time their refugee status changed to migrant status. Most became Australian citizens to protect themselves from Soviet authorities. But, for some, citizenship was not enough: one elderly Lithuanian couple were so afraid of being repatriated to the Soviet Union that they lived in hiding for 28 years in a cave near Sydney.[18]

Some of the older migrants I interviewed confirmed that they lived for years with the fear of being captured by KGB agents in Australia. Afraid to visit Lithuania, they lived a tenuous existence between the two countries – Australia physically and Lithuania emotionally. Their sense of living 'in-between' was exacerbated by hostile attitudes among Australians. Public attitudes were not welcoming, with refugees (like other migrants) made to feel inferior by being asked to speak English in the presence of Australians.[19] Those who completed their schooling in Australia were laughed at and made to feel uncomfortable for what they ate at school, such as bacon or salami sandwiches.[20] Many tried to hide their lunches and eat in secret, or begged their parents to make the same sandwiches that other children ate. One of my respondents explained that she felt privileged at school because students always wished to play with her and her friends never laughed at her thick sandwiches. Nonetheless, she felt that something was not right, and she used to ask her mother to cut bread in thinner slices. 'When my mother was in hospital,' she recalled, 'my father made me take a chicken thigh to school. I ate it on the way to school not to be embarrassed. I wanted to be like other kids and the best way was to try not to be different.'[21]

The discrimination was not always overt. 'It was subtle', according to one respondent. 'When I say subtle, it wasn't in the open. People discouraged you from speaking in your own language.' Later he experienced professional discrimination, and would never forgot how, when he went for promotion, a colleague advised: 'To get a job you have to be three times better than the Aussie.'[22] One Australian woman married to a Lithuanian was with a group of Lithuanians who were all verbally abused by a car load of Australians while crossing the road: 'Get back to where you bloody come from, you bloody wogs, and get off the bloody road so we can drive our bloody car.'[23] One respondent would regularly question British migrants on the pressure to assimilate into the mainstream. 'How about you, can you forget England?' she asked. The British migrants were surprised that the question was even posed, as they assumed assimilation only applied to non-Anglo-Celts.[24]

Despite a policy of assimilation, in reality it was difficult to assimilate because of the many barriers erected between mainstream society and ethnic minorities. Newcomers were constantly addressed as New Australians or DPs – even though, according to a 1947 survey, 45 per cent of Australians did not know what the term Displaced Persons meant. Another 23 per cent knew what the term meant but were not in favour of Australia taking them in.[25]

Most of the postwar generation Lithuanians I interviewed had been called 'bloody Balts' or 'bloody New Australians'. Working class Australians, with whom Lithuanians often mixed, were suspicious of what they perceived as a 'cheap labour pool.' To others, Lithuanians were either Nazis or agents of the Russian secret service. Some of the Baltic people who settled in Tasmania were looked upon as if they 'had come from the moon' and were constantly stared at. Although postwar Baltic refugees had the required 'Nordic' appearance, they were made to feel different and they felt different. Hoping eventually to return to Lithuania, many resisted the official program of assimilation and 'threw themselves wholeheartedly into the activities of the national associations'.[26]

### *Age and education upon arrival*

The initial Australian intake of 843 Balts in 1947 had been restricted to single males and females between 18 and 40 years of age[27] – a pattern that persisted with the postwar Lithuanian group from the late 1940s, the great majority of whom were 30 or younger on arrival. The Australian policy was to bring out wives and children only after the men found suitable accommodation. There were exceptions: the first ship from Germany to Australia, the *General Stuart Heintzelman*, brought 417 Lithuanian men and 22 women. But they were very much in the minority. Some of the Lithuanian men who arrived on ships after 1947 had left their wives and children in Soviet-occupied Lithuania and, when it proved impossible to bring them to Australia, lived in *de facto* relationships or married local girls. Again, there were exceptions, such as Robertas Kasparas who, after enormous effort, was reunited with his wife Marija after 20 years, though their four children were forced to stay in Soviet Lithuania. For some, even temporary separation from their families was unbearable. Ben Beržanskas complained that the Australian authorities did not allow his wife and one-year-old daughter to come to Australia for nine months after his arrival, and they were left behind in Germany to face starvation – the policy being to bring out wives and children only after the men found suitable accommodation. The men who arrived on board the *Svalbard* in 1948 signed a petition to the Australian Immigration Department asking for their families to be sent to Australia on the next transport. However, two-thirds of the petitioners had to wait almost a year to see their families. Only in the 1950s were most of the families reunited and the balance between men and women reestablished.[28]

Most of the single postwar generation Lithuanians did not speak enough English to get acquainted with local girls, and remained isolated. According to Egon F. Kunz's *Displaced persons: Calwell's new Australians,* marriage to Australian women was particularly unwelcome by Estonians, Latvians and Lithuanians, because the smaller ethnic communities were determined not to mix their culture and language. Marrying an outsider risked being alienated from their communities. At the same time, Australians did not want their daughters to marry so-called New Australians. Margaret Bartkevičius remembers how her father was very much against her marriage to a 'German', and in general regarded new arrivals as having poor moral values.[29]

Among the postwar Lithuanians I interviewed, more than 10 per cent of were under ten years of age when they came to Australia. Too young to attend school in Lithuania, many had begun their education in European DP camps, followed by the challenge of continuing in assimilationist Australia. Among older respondents, a quarter had attended high school and more than 20 per cent post-secondary school before coming to Australia. According to Kunz, 63 per cent of Lithuanian males aged 19 and 60 arrived in Australia with only primary and 6 per cent with tertiary education, compared with 48 per cent of Australian males with only primary and 2 per cent with tertiary education. Although the education of many was disrupted by war, they were able to pursue their studies in DP camps and later in Australia.[30] Indeed, in the German refugee camps the Baltic refugees had unprecedented educational opportunities at all levels, thanks to the presence of teachers, artists, musicians, theatre directors and tradesmen among their number. They had access to two universities, first at Hamburg and then in Pinneberg, opened for DPs. The Baltic DPs University had eight faculties with 1,200 students, taught by 170 professors. Of 76 University graduates 53 were Latvians, 16 Lithuanians, and seven Estonians. In addition to schooling activities, many were involved in theatre, choir and ballet performances. Others learned new trades which later helped them to establish themselves in Australia.[31]

### *Compulsory two-year contract and the aftermath*

In Australia arriving DPs were tied to a two-year compulsory contract to fill positions locals did not want. Generally, postwar refugees were divided into only two categories: labourers and domestics. Bureaucratic processes within the Commonwealth Department of Labour and National Service determined what kind of work DPs should do. For instance, 'unskilled labourers' requiring 'no special skills' were used in connection with the electricity supply at the Yallourn Open Cut Mine in Victoria.[32] The compulsory contract denied highly-qualified professionals the opportunity to practise their professions.[33] Despite a great shortage of doctors in Australia, Lithuanian doctors were used to build bridges and work at the railways. The government's narrow-mindedness disappointed newcomers and at the same time disadvantaged the Australian labour market.[34] The Australian Military Mission in Berlin superior officer recommended that the DP doctors be recruited only as 'qualified medical orderlies.' The perception at the time was that 'European degrees had no value, since everyone knew they could be bought on the European black market.'[35] In 1949, the 60 Lithuanian men and women assigned to Concord Military Hospital as wardsmen, cleaners, domestics and laundry hands included six doctors. At the end of their contract, they were invited to practise medicine in Papua New Guinea only. On return to Australia, in order to register as doctors they had to repeat part of their medical studies at an Australian university. It has been estimated that by the end of 1951, out of some 300 male and 100 female overseas trained DP doctors in Australia, only 12 per cent obtained medical appointments.[36]

Not only were Lithuanians dispersed around Australia, but they also worked on difficult and dangerous projects in factories, coalmines and railways. Some 400 Lithuanian men were allocated to Newcastle and Wollongong steel mills, while 25 dug a tunnel through the mountains at Guthega, in the Snowy Mountains. At Lake Bolac, 12 Lithuanians worked in a linen factory and 20 in the Onkaparinga Woollen Mill.[37] The result was that highly educated people lost their self-esteem and felt disillusioned with the treatment they received from the authorities and the status they had to occupy in their new environment. With such little encouragement to identify as Australians, it is not surprising that so many migrants focused instead on what they were familiar with – an independent Lithuanian identity.

Australia's loss was the Lithuanian community's gain. Among the Lithuanian refugees completing the compulsory two-year contract as labourers were musicians such as Albertas Čelna, Kazimieras Kavaliauskas, Mečislovas Kymantas and Vaclovas Šimkus. Unable to find employment as musicians, they devoted their spare time to the Lithuanian community's cultural life. On her arrival in Australia in 1949, one of my interviewees worked as a nursing aide in a dental department. Although fully qualified as a dentist in Germany, she could not obtain a position as a dentist and had to begin repeating the dental surgery course in 1957. After considerable time and effort, she was able to open her own dental practice in 1960, where she worked for 25 years. Like her compatriot musicians, in all that time she remained closely involved in the cultural life of the Lithuanian community.[38]

After the two-year compulsory contract period expired, many Lithuanians were better able to establish themselves. Some pursued higher education as a direct outcome of their educational start in Lithuania and DP camps. Others completed primary or secondary education, or attended trade school or courses.[39] But the fate of many of the so-called 'Reffos' was to be confined to second class roles. By the time they were eligible for Australian citizenship some were ready to leave. By 1958, about 2,000 (20 per cent of those living in Australia) had emigrated to the US. For the qualified professionals decided to remain in Australia, many found that by the late 1960s their employment prospects had still not markedly improved. Of the Lithuanian males who had arrived in Australia 1949–50, by 1970 only one-third of 257 former professionals were reestablished in their original professions, and one half were still blue-collar workers.[40]

Of the 8,000 Lithuanians remaining in Australia in the 1960s, approximately 2,500 had settled in suburban Sydney, 1,500 in Melbourne and 1,200 in Adelaide.[41] The rest chose between Canberra, Newcastle, Geelong and Hobart. Most appear to have been able to secure employment after their two-year contract, perhaps reflecting their young age and the demand for labour in Australia's developing economy. But relative success extinguished neither the memories of the past nor the desire to one day return to their homeland.

As refugees, they had left behind home and belongings, family members, friends and loved ones. Among the people I interviewed, most found it difficult – certainly for the first ten years – to adjust to their new environment, and they lived with a hope of return. Homesickness and imagining the lost homeland preoccupied the thoughts of many. One recalled that her homesickness started while living in Germany in 1944, and for four years she constantly cried for her homeland. Another had not seen her homeland from the time of her departure for Australia, but her homesickness had never lessened and she passed her love of the homeland onto her students at the Lithuanian Saturday school. During one of the school concerts she asked them to describe Lithuania: 'It is a fairytale country, so beautiful that one cannot even imagine it', students replied in chorus. 'I was shaken by their answers, in the sense that my students had no idea of the real Lithuania', she said. 'I think we paint the wrong picture to our children and mislead them.'[42]

This mixture of fantasy with reality gave rise to a constant comparison between the homeland and the host-land – a never-ending weighing of the level of satisfaction or dissatisfaction with living in the diaspora. Like the Saturday school children who had no direct experience of Lithuania, many postwar generation Lithuanians idealised their homeland, or the homeland of their parents. One person I interviewed remembered how, during her visit to Lithuania in the 1990s, she realised 'things were distorted slightly in memory and were not exactly as recorded.' She was greatly disappointed with her birthplace, and distressed to discover that her birth town Tauragė looked so unkempt, 'as if it was still the war zone. That's how neglected it was.' Nostalgia for place was conflated with regret for lost childhood and youth. Back at her high school she found a group of students having a party. 'So, they sat around the table, they sang, they played, and I cried. My son held my hands as if I was a child. That's nostalgia for you.'[43]

Another person I interviewed explained that homesickness was common among postwar Lithuanian nationals 'because Lithuania wasn't free. I think it is different now; they can go for a visit any time' – and he gave as an example his own mother flying to Lithuania for her first return visit in her 80s. Another was adamant that she did not wish to hold onto her parents' feelings forever. On the one hand she agreed that all migrants feel homesick for a time, particularly if they fled their birthplace. On the other hand, 'a decent lifestyle compensates. Hunger is more detrimental than homesickness.'[44] The different intensity of mourning for the old and adapting to the new reminds us that we are dealing, not just with an abstraction, but with *real* people who cover the full range of human experience and response. Of those I interviewed, only 3 per cent wanted to return to Lithuania to die, with a further 7 per cent undecided. The majority wanted to remain in Australia, citing economic or other reasons.[45] But such statistics convey only part of the story, and trying to compare the intensity of personal longings for a lost past or the depth and impact of homesickness glosses over the ongoing trauma and grief of individuals like the woman who constantly cried over four years for her lost homeland. While it is clear that people reacted differently to their situation, it is also clear that, as a group, postwar Lithuanians suffered greatly from culture shock.

## Haunting of the Soviet past

Even after eventually integrating into the Australian mainstream, some continued to relive the nightmare of the past. One person I interviewed just felt lucky to have escaped so far away that nobody could reach her. 'From the first day I was so happy in Australia that I forgot everything. I just switched off absolutely, physically and morally, and would never swap back.' But she still lived with her memories of the communists in Lithuania and of what had happened to her family, all of whom were deported to Siberia:

> The communists took all my family and my brother was sent straight away from high school to jail. My stepfather was taken to jail. They came into our house just like in *Doctor Zhivago* and we had to sleep in a passage, then at night time we had to

> open the window and to steal our own clothes because there were not enough to take with us. We had to leave everything behind. It was terrible, such a hell.[46]

Another feared that she would not survive interrogation or deportation given her poor health. 'Everyone's life was under threat. Not only teachers and other intellectuals, but also farmers and young men were deported.'[47]

For one interviewee, it was people like her parents who suffered the most. Her father, having been a good provider all his life, suddenly found himself, with his wife and children, leaving Lithuania and ending up in a refugee camp in Denmark, where he died of lung cancer. 'This type of emotional loss was terrible. And this is what the Soviets did to our nation. People drastically suffered.'

> Just imagine all those families. We were quite lucky, our whole family was together, never got lost on the way. Hundreds from Lithuania got lost. 'Have you seen my mother?' 'Have you seen my sister?' 'Have you seen my brother?' It was incredible; they never found each other because it was too hard to find.[48]

In my own case, my grandparents were separated by the war in Germany and my mother, then nine years of age, was forced to beg for food in order to feed her three sisters and my grandmother – an experience she still remembers with great embarrassment. She recalls not being able to openly beg, just standing at the doors until people came out and shared some food with her.

Another person I interviewed had spent 1945 to 1947 in Siberia. After returning to Lithuania she was constantly followed and interrogated by KGB agents. Her husband was living in Australia and eventually she received permission to join him. The condition was that she had to leave her daughter behind. This she could not accept and she stayed in Lithuanian until 1967, when she and her daughter were finally allowed to leave for Australia. Police escorted mother and daughter to Moscow airport. 'You will never be able to return', she was told.[49]

Such memories cannot be erased and certainly impact on health and wellbeing. A descendent of postwar Lithuanian refugees witnessed how the older generation of Lithuanians suffered. 'They were dreadfully homesick when they came here', she observed, 'because nobody knew if they would be able to go back, if anybody would be able to visit. I think a lot of the illness of older people in the community is a consequence of leaving their country. Many people left their children behind, mothers, fathers. And I think it's a massive trauma.' As a young girl she had become used to seeing older Lithuanian men looking sad and lonely. 'They would gather at Lithuanian House and drink heavily in order to forget their sorrows.' Another postwar refugee descendent recalled young men drinking at her father's house: 'They were reminiscing, [and for me] that was an opportunity, just sitting there and listening and observing these people going back into the past.' She witnessed her parents' post-traumatic stress, with both 'reverting back to living in the war.' Her mother was just 17 when she came to Australia and she always longed to return to Lithuania. Her father, believing he had no relatives left, felt no need to return – until he received a letter confirming they were alive. He began thinking of visiting the homeland. The return was a traumatic experience, possibly triggering his wife's heart attack. 'It was all too much for her', their daughter recalled. 'The lake that was there had been filled in, the forest had been cut down and the farm had been destroyed.'[50]

## *Mental health issues*

Research into psychiatric disorders in East European refugees in Australia confirms that Lithuanians and other Balts fared somewhat better than other Eastern European DPs, who exhibited double the rate of alcoholism and suicide compared with locals. It has been argued that Baltic immigrants' mental health was affected by their double acculturation within their new environment in Germany and again in Australia, as well as their unintentional emigration circumstances from the Baltic countries and separation from their families and friends.[51] But being relatively better off than other Eastern European refugees does not detract from the suffering that Lithuanians and other Baltic refugees in Australia endured. According to Egon Kunz, alcoholism was particularly high among Baltic refugees, who turned to alcohol for various reasons – though a common theme is separation from loved ones. One young man in Tasmania developed a drinking problem because he could not forget how his best friend's head was blown off by a shell. Another man hanged himself because his wife and two of his children were exiled to Siberia, and two other children had died during the war. Other stories are less dramatic, but there is a pattern of single men in the early 1950s becoming heavy drinkers. Talented people, unable to adjust, and turning to alcohol to lessen the pain.[52] In the circumstances, it is not surprising that something approaching a siege mentality took hold in sections of the Lithuanian community. As we shall see, this had positive, as well as negative, outcomes.

## *Maintaining* lietuvybė

Lithuanian activities initiated in DP camps in Europe were taken up in assimilationist Australia. Song festivals and sporting activities, well maintained in Germany, came to form the core of Lithuanian existence in Australia. The majority of refugees had grown up in independent Lithuania (1918–40), where cultural and sporting activities were greatly encouraged, and the desire for such self-expression remained strong after their detachment from Lithuania. In 1945, a Lithuanian community was formed at the Hanau (Hannover) camp in the German province of Hesse. The Lithuanians organised camp police and a post office, and journalists established three Lithuanian language newspapers, as well as a magazine for children, all printed by hand press requiring its own unique set of skills. Cultural activities spread around the camps of Germany and Austria. In 1947, the first Song Festival was held in Wűrzburg, with some 400 singers taking part in the event during their exile in Germany. Sporting activities such as basketball, table tennis and volleyball were similarly organised.[53]

In Australia, Lithuanians gravitated towards the Lithuanian Houses or Clubs, which were, and still are, used to accommodate Lithuanian weekend schools, community meetings, theatre performances, and concerts, and are open for choir, theatre and folk dancing rehearsals free of charge. The activities bound Lithuanians together for mutual support and gave them an abiding sense of belonging. A Credit Union, Talka, was founded in Melbourne and expanded over the years to other states. At a time when most Lithuanian nationals lacked capital, Talka helped them to establish themselves in Australia, and the profits subsidised Lithuanian activities.[54]

The Australian Lithuanian Foundation (ALF) also raised funds through voluntary donations and legacies. Over 40 years the ALF spent some $11 million dollars for the maintenance of *lietuvybė*. Cordial relations were established with other ethnic groups and close ties forged with the Latvian and Estonian communities. All states could boast a Baltic Women's Association, a Baltic Youth Action Group, a Baltic Council and a Federal Executive of Baltic Councils. The Baltic Councils organised peaceful demonstrations, ecumenical services, and Commemoration Days to mark the mass deportation of people from the Baltic countries.[55]

The community's cultural life was sustained by the spare time efforts of the postwar Lithuanians. Their active involvement in the community enhanced both their social status and their self-esteem. A cleaner or a factory worker by day could be a community leader by night. Perhaps this compensated for the exclusion at the heart of assimilation. It also reflected an underlying desire on the part of many to maintain a Lithuanian national cultural identity in order eventually to return to Lithuania with a preserved Lithuanian identity intact.

The preservation of Lithuanian culture, free from the contaminating influence of communism, also motivated the Roman Catholic Church. Over many centuries Roman Catholicism had played an important role in the lives of Lithuanians. Its rituals and customs had become part of national identity. In Australia, postwar Lithuanians were quick to establish the Lithuanian Catholic Association of St Kazimieras at Bathurst immigration camp in 1948. In 1954 it was reorganised into the Australian Lithuanian Catholic Federation, bringing together all Lithuanian Catholic Associations across the nation. The Federation saw itself 'in the forefront of the fight against the godlessness of Communism.'[56] Lithuanian Catholics in Australia were wary of dialogue with the Soviet-occupied homeland and believed that, though exiled so far from home, they had a better opportunity to save the Catholic religion of their country than those still in Lithuania. By initiating national commemorations, founding libraries and publishing Catholic newspapers, the Federation helped to keep the Lithuanian language as well as religious traditions alive. Lithuanian priests playing the role of social workers, interpreters and teachers at Lithuanian weekend schools contributed significantly to maintaining a high profile for the Church. Every two years Federation members would come together to discuss ways of preserving Catholicism within the community. In July 1959, Archbishop Romolo Carboni commemorated the tenth anniversary of the Federation by declaring that, while Lithuanians needed to adapt to the requirements of a new country, they also needed to maintain their beautiful traditions. 'Preserve your beautiful language, as it would be a shame to forget it. Every Lithuanian boy and girl must know his/her father's language and the history of their name country.'[57] Adapting to the requirements of a new country and at the same time preserving their language was bound to be a difficult balance to achieve, especially in an aggressively monolingual society like Australia.

Ultimately, as a later chapter will describe, successfully preserving their language of birth would itself be a barrier to reconnecting with their country of birth. As one of my interviewees lamented: 'In Australia we were able to preserve our pure language. Unfortunately now the language and other human qualities in the homeland are not the same.' Another reminisced: 'Although we left our homeland a long time ago, we still live in a prewar Lithuania and remember it the way we left it.'[58] As we shall see, this has important implications for the Lithuanian language. But before discussing those, let us turn to the situation of the Lithuanians who came to Australia after 1970, who also brought with them memories – though of the postwar Soviet system rather than an independent Lithuania.

CHAPTER 3

# Reconstructing 'Lithuania' in Australia: second wave migrants

## *1970s–1980s*

Second wave migration from Lithuania to Australia was much smaller than the immediate postwar refugee migration. According to Australian government data, from 1970 to 1975 the number of Lithuanian settlers was just 35, and in the period 1991 to 2000 it was 152. While figures are not available for the intervening period – when Lithuanians were recorded as Soviet citizens – the 2006 Census indicates that 174 people born in Lithuania settled in Australia from 1970 to 1989. The number of Lithuanian-born settlers arriving in Australia from 1990 to 2006 increased to 474 – totalling 648 arrivals from 1970 to 2006. Migration during the period 1970–89 was associated with the process of de-Stalinisation and Gorbachev's *perestroika*, when fewer restrictions on non-Russians meant that a limited number of nationals were allowed to leave Lithuania. Like postwar refugees before them, these later Lithuanian migrants positioned their sense of national and cultural identity in terms of their understanding of the past and their hopes for the future. The difference was that their understanding was refracted through the lens of living under communism, and did not include the imperative felt by postwar refugees to preserve Lithuanian culture free from the contaminating Soviet influence.

There has been very little research into second wave Lithuanian migrants, and the information that follows, based on 45 questionnaire returns and 23 interviews with second wave migrants, is the most comprehensive research to date. The interviews canvassed reasons for migration, educational achievement, relationship with place of birth and settlement difficulties in Australia – as well as issues of hybridisation and creolisation of Lithuanian language and identity in Australia and continuing connections with their birthplace. The survey does not claim to be scientific, but as the most comprehensive analysis to date it provides a valuable 'snapshot' of a cross-section of the community.

Nearly 70 per cent of questionnaire respondents arrived after 1989, and of the 23 interviewees only one person had arrived before the 1980s. The 1970s were the years of attempted revival of national consciousness in Lithuania – with events like the self-immolation of the youth Romas Kalanta and the ordeal of the sailor Simas Kudirka in trying to escape his Soviet ship – and in the repressive political climate it was not easy to obtain a visa to leave Soviet Lithuania.

The restrictions eased in the late 1980s and early 1990s. By 1980, with the slight lifting of the iron curtain, Lithuanian artists were for the first time able to come to Australia to visit Australian Lithuanians – albeit as part of a Russian group.[1] By the late 1980s, Moscow's attempt to 'restructure' the non-Russian nationalities resulted in a 'national reawakening' among the Baltic states,[2] with Lithuania loosening its ties to the Soviet Union before gaining its independence in 1991. In the 1990s the newly independent states, including Lithuania, experienced a new wave of migration, with most migrants aged between 20 and 40 – though the ages covered a much wider range than the average suggests. Similarly, there was a range of reasons for migration. One of the people I interviewed believed that 'everyone has a right to fulfil his/her needs.' For others, Australia provided 'more opportunities to express yourself', and 'in Australia one has a perfect chance for good personal life.'[3]

According to Department of Immigration and Citizenship of Australia (DIMA) statistics, more than 60 per cent of Lithuanian-born arrivals in the period 1991 to 2000 settled in Australia under family migration, joining relatives already living here. Sixty per cent of the people I interviewed came to Australia to marry, the remaining 40 per cent coming on the migration scheme for professionals or to join their families. More than 20 per cent had married Australians in Lithuania, though it was not always easy, especially in the 1970s.[4] After her marriage to her Australian Lithuanian husband in 1974, one interviewee did not know if the Soviet authorities would allow her to leave. They did, but only after one and a half years. Another faced difficulties after her 1980 marriage to an Australian Macedonian, with KGB agents inquiring of relatives and close friends whether her marriage was the genuine reason for emigration, and the person processing her application in Vilnius when she was pregnant calling her a 'bitch'. Another obtained her departure visa just five months after marrying an Australian Lithuanian in 1987, though her husband-to-be – who had come to Lithuania to upgrade his qualifications – was regularly questioned by KGB agents as to his motives for staying in Lithuania. After the marriage, it was safer for her to travel on a visitor's visa to Australia, where she was able to apply for permanent residency.[5]

Forty per cent of interviewees married their future partners in Australia, after going through the process of filling in forms and waiting – often for many months – for their applications for permanent residency to be approved. In my own case, I had to wait for eight months to receive permanent residency while my wedding photos and video were checked out by Immigration officials in Geelong. The officials separately interviewed my husband and me to compare our stories on how and where we met to determine whether our marriage was legitimate. Because I had arrived in Australia for a six-week visit, my visitor's visa had to be extended after meeting my husband-to-be. After we married, it was a tense time for both of us, and I was convinced that the Australian or the Soviet Immigration authorities would request my return to Lithuania. Close to 30 per cent of interviewees who married in Australia initially came to visit their relatives and only later found their partners and married.[6]

### *Education and professional skills*

Second wave Lithuanian migrants covered a wider age range than the earlier settlers, but it was their different personal experiences as Soviet or post-Soviet citizens that really distinguished them from their compatriots. Of the 45 respondents to my questionnaire, nearly 70 per cent came to Australia with a tertiary degree. This reflected the goal of public education in the Soviet Union: to prepare highly educated, physically healthy 'and active builders of the communist society, brought up on the ideas of Marxism-Leninism', and to 'ensure the development and satisfaction of the spiritual and intellectual needs of Soviet man.'[7] In 1913, 118,000 children in Lithuania were attending elementary schools. By 1970, the number had grown to 562,000. In the summer of 1973, compulsory eight-year schooling was introduced, and higher educational opportunities in the Soviet Union more than tripled between 1953 and 1978, with more than 19 students per 1,000 of the population having higher education by the late 1970s.[8]

Most of my questionnaire respondents arrived in Australia as professionals, though qualifications were not in themselves always sufficient to secure appropriate employment, with 60 per cent unable to practise their profession in Australia. While about half did not specify whether they undertook further studies on arrival, 40 per cent indicated that they had repeated their studies, half of that figure undertaking post-secondary and tertiary degrees. The remaining 10 per cent did not do any studies in Australia. Of the interviewees, 50 per cent did not continue with their education, 40 per cent did tertiary studies, with the remaining 10 per cent completing different courses.[9]

Nearly half of the questionnaire respondents worked as skilled and unskilled labourers in Australia. Out of those, over 20 per cent were able to find professional employment, though not necessarily in their previous profession. For other 20 per cent unable to find any employment, Australia was hardly 'a land of opportunity'. Of the interviewees, 70 per cent did not work in their profession. Many with higher degrees expressed dissatisfaction at their qualifications being wasted. One was unable to find work as an economist, and regretted that since arriving in Australia she could not return to study or find a job due to her lack of English. Another, a librarian in Lithuania, did not work because she felt an outsider within and outside the Lithuanian community. One, a geographer, ran his own computer business. A highly qualified academic worked as a sessional teacher.[10] In my own case, although my qualifications were fully recognised in Australia, I was unable to work as a choir conductress, and conducting became a hobby rather than professional employment, with administrative work my main source of income.

Other respondents had different experiences. A number felt happy in Australia because of their successful marriages, or because they *did* find work in their professions. Some were well established in Australia and due to their secure financial situation could visit their relatives in Lithuania whenever they wished. One regarded Australia as a wonderful country with a colourful landscape and an abundance of space. For another, life was much better here than in Lithuania.[11]

## *Consequences of resettlement*

More than half of the respondents strongly agreed or agreed that their expectations on arrival had been met. A quarter were uncertain, and close to 15 per cent disagreed or strongly disagreed. Some admitted that their expectations had been unrealistic. One expressed disappointment with Australian culture, the education system and the building industry, all of which in his view were well behind European standards. Another had expected that settling in the host country would have been easier and faster. One, at 48 years of age with very limited English and a shortage of money, found it a constant struggle to survive, and never realised her initial hopes. For another respondent who also came to Australia in her 40s, it was too late to start a new life.[12]

Many respondents were dissatisfied because they could not find jobs in their profession, with their qualifications often regarded with suspicion or not recognised in Australia.[13] But while many recent migrants struggled to find employment in their field of expertise, competing with local economists, musicians or engineers, others came to the realisation that their previous profession was simply not useful or relevant in Australia. This was my own experience, as I confronted the reality that, unlike in Lithuania, conducting a choir in Australia as a profession was simply not an option.

Their post-settlement experiences were reflected in respondents' views on whether or not they would recommend emigration to other Lithuanians. More than half were either uncertain or would not recommend it, compared with 40 per cent who would recommend or strongly recommend it. Age, profession, English proficiency and availability of jobs all featured as factors. One respondent lamented that that 'detachment from your roots makes you feel nostalgic and unbalanced.' Another associated his settlement difficulties with earlier 'postwar migrants not offering any support, while recent migrants themselves are unable to help each other.' The experience of one led him to believe that 'we must live where we were born, with our language and traditions, surrounded by our close families and friends. Lithuanians belong to Lithuania!'[14]

Others displayed more positive attitudes towards emigration. Comments included that life in Australia was much better than in Lithuania, that 'Australia is a country where one can always find a job and live well', and that there were better opportunities in Australia to express oneself. One respondent admitted feeling happier knowing that he was able to return to Lithuania at any time. He chose to live in Australia for a 'practical reason', namely marriage, and considered himself psychologically ready to make a personal transition from one country to another. He had no regrets in making this kind of decision. Another admitted that she had dreamed about Australia since she was a little girl. Not allowed by the Soviet authorities to visit her relatives in Australia, she finally obtained a visa in 1989 and joined her aunt. She still found Australia a fascinating place in which to live and she felt happy here – though at the same time she constantly thought of her family left behind. For others there were no such regrets: 'Nowadays', one remarked, 'recent migrants arrive in Australia of their own will, therefore taking responsibility for their decision. They become responsible for their fate.'[15]

Taking personal responsibility does not, however, rule out the pervasive experience of homesickness. All migrants bring with them personal memories of the homeland – though the precise nature of an individual's memories is determined by their particular circumstances in deciding to migrate. Some circumstances are shared, others are uniquely personal. As one respondent put it, he remembered 'Lithuania not as a country on a map but for specific facts and events, for my dreams about the future and for spending my youth with my close friends.'[16] Some regarded homesickness a 'natural phenomenon, an unavoidable part of emigration', an 'individual feeling associated with personal life experiences.' Another respondent, who had lived in Australia since 1987, tried to suppress her homesickness for the unwelcome memories it evoked. Her life in Lithuania had been plagued by constant KGB interrogation, and for seven years she had attempted to emigrate overseas. Finally, in 1987, the Soviet authorities granted her permission to leave Lithuania, but would not allow her to take any documents, including her (Soviet) passport, birth certificate or study diploma. It was awful, she recalled, 'to leave your homeland without anything.'[17]

Feelings of uncertainty occupied the thoughts of many. One referred to the difficulty of leading a double life – living in one place, while thinking of another. She felt psychologically divided between Lithuania and Australia. Although she appreciated Australia for its endless opportunities, her homeland was, and always would be, closer to her heart. Another felt disillusioned because she did not have the opportunity to work in her profession and she missed her close family. 'I live here', she confided, 'because of my duty to my husband and my children, hiding away my secret desires to return. Psychologically it is very difficult to cope with loss of the homeland.'[18]

Others were even more trenchant in expressing their disillusionment. Not only was her life in Lithuania better, declared one, but in Australia 'everything is unpleasant and foreign: language, traditions, people.' Another could never return to Lithuania, but was also unhappy in Australia, where everything displeased her: the people, the culture and the surroundings.

'I am at the stage', she admitted, 'where I could never be happy, here nor back home.'[19]

Homesickness works in reverse as well. Some respondents reported feeling nostalgic for Australia when visiting their birthplace – missing their homeland while living in Australia, and during their visits to Lithuania missing the Australian way of life. The result for some was that they were simply not sure where home is: 'I do not know where I would go next. Would I stay in Australia, return to Lithuania or go elsewhere? There are many things I miss. However mostly I long for my homeland and my loved ones. It is a big question where my next home would be.'[20]

## *Evaluating the Soviet past*

The reality for most second wave migrants was that they lived between two worlds: the lost past and the present. Their double existence between two countries situated them in what Homi Bhabha has described as the 'third space', where the previous homeland identity had become dislocated and dismantled. At the same time, they had adopted some elements of an Australian identity – a hybridised space, neither *there* nor *here*. Their in-between existence, their life in the third space encompassing two countries, two cultures, two eras, made recent migrants feel different or 'other' in their host country. Like the earlier postwar Lithuanian nationals, for some the hope of return persisted.

These ambivalent views are tied up with conflicting memories of the Soviet past. Half of the interviewees recalled negative aspects of the Soviet system: inheriting a 'low morale' and bad economic situation, being obliged to study the Russian language and the history of communism, learning Russian propaganda at the expense of Lithuanian history, Lenin represented as a father figure and the Soviet as the homeland from kindergarten on, becoming passive and just waiting indifferently for a better life. Still waiting for things to change for the better even many years after Lithuanian independence, rather than taking responsibility for bringing about change.[21]

Some associated the Soviet regime with terror, deportations, constraints and assimilation. During the years of Soviet occupation, one maintained, Lithuanians lost their sense of pride and justice, with economic conditions setting Lithuania back 100 years. Another would rather have spent her time reading apolitical literature than being forced to learn Marxism-Leninism during her studies of music. Ostensibly made up of 15 republics with their own customs and traditions, under the Soviet system Russian culture prevailed and Russian language was obligatory. In contrast, the Lithuanian history book was 'very thin', and there was nowhere to go to learn about the Lithuanian past.[22]

Many commented on how the Soviet period bred indifference and passivity, with no sense of competition and no incentive to work harder than anybody else. People were not encouraged to show their talents, to be creative or to think independently.[23] As Stanley Vytas Vardys has noted, Lithuanian intellectuals who 'rejected Socialist realism as the sole artistic criterion' and spread 'objectivist, apolitical principles of aesthetics', were exposed to public scrutiny and humiliation. The fate of the prominent literary critic Vytautas Kubilius was typical: forced 'to make a public confession of ideological errors', he had to publicly apologise 'to those who were insulted by [his] lack of tact and inconsiderate cleverness.'[24]

The experience of individual insignificance within the Soviet system was well-captured by Russian poet Vladimir Mayakovsky:

*The individual: who needs him?*
*The voice of one man is weaker than a squeak.*
*Who will listen to it? Not even a wife ...*
*The Party is the all-encompassing hurricane,*
*Fused from voices, soft and quiet ...*
*Misfortune befalls a man when he's alone.*
*Grief comes to one man, for one alone is not a warrior.*
*Every person is his master,*
*Whether sturdy, or even weak...*
*The individual is nonsense,*
*The individual is nothing ...*[25]

The overwhelming majority of recent migrants who featured in my research would agree that the individual was suppressed under communism. Yet a quarter noted the resilience of the Lithuanian culture. According to one, while the Soviet system encouraged all citizens of the USSR to follow the communist line, the culture of individual countries was not entirely suppressed. Yes, Lithuanians did sing about Lenin and build sculptures reflecting the Soviet ideology, but 'the songs were sung in Lithuanian, and were often accompanied by dances that expressed the Lithuanian national character.'[26]

Another interviewee made a similar point, noting how in the Soviet era Lithuanian culture was stifled and isolated, provincial and full of falsehoods in many areas. 'However, not all Lithuanian culture developed during the Soviet era should be regarded as 'Soviet culture' … some of it has nothing to do with the Soviet ideology and was created despite the Soviet rule, not because of it.'[27]

About 20 per cent of interviewees regarded the Soviet era positively. The ideas of communism were very good, one argued, adding that there was nothing wrong with teaching Marxism-Leninism and learning the Russian language, as one can never have enough education and should be open-minded towards new languages and ideas. The Soviet era did not leave the deeply harming effects on Lithuania as postwar Lithuanian migrants living in the diaspora imagined. The effects depended on one's personality and one's own attempt to stay Lithuanian. During the Soviet era, some Lithuanians continued to celebrate forbidden religious holidays such as Christmas or Easter in secret, and because of that secrecy these celebrations were even more popular. 'The more the Soviets tried to stop religious events, the more people wanted to celebrate!'[28]

A number of interviewees recalled how during the Soviet period song, dance and other festivals helped to maintain the Lithuanian language, culture and art. While Lithuanian literature had to comply with the rules of Social Realism, poetry had to be politicised. One respondent confirmed that even love poetry had to have a 'political colouring'. Some remembered the years of the Soviet system with pride, when many theatres were built and books published. Books were so popular that people would stand in long queues to buy a favourite. With a centralised cultural system and cultural houses staffed by paid professionals, visitors enjoyed high quality entertainment. In contrast, with Lithuania free and independent, it was impossible to find the works of the Lithuanian writer Maironis (1862–1932), which were always available during the Soviet era. The availability of national literature and access to professional entertainment were attributed to the highly organised cultural life during the Soviet era. There were, however, limits. As Richard Krickus noted, Krushchev and Brezhnev allowed Soviet Republics to publish books and depict their cultures in plays and films, only if these 'national achievements' were under Soviet control.[29]

Another positive aspect of the Soviet period noted by some respondents was that education was free and one did not have to pay for one's schooling, unlike in Australia. One respondent was impressed with the Soviet education system's continuing influence on people's views, intellect and personal qualities such as honesty and warmth.[30]

The range of views among second wave of Lithuanian migrants is striking, with pessimistic and optimistic appraisals of the Soviet system competing – sometimes even in the one person's mind! With such varying views, it is difficult to categorise second wave Lithuanian migrants as one cohesive group. They arrived in Australia for many different personal reasons. Some experienced alienation in their host country and wanted to return to Lithuania. Others found acceptance and created a new home. On one point, however, there was agreement: most wanted to maintain their Lithuanian identity in Australia.

## *Maintaining Soviet Lithuanian identity*

Eighty per cent of my respondents either agreed or strongly agreed that the maintenance of the Lithuanian national and cultural identity in Australia was important. The remaining 20 per cent were uncertain. The common view among interviewees was that 'we must always remember the language and traditions of the country we were born in.' 'We are born and will remain

Lithuanians, no matter where we live.' Lithuanians need to maintain their identity 'for the sake of their children.' The uniqueness of 'Lithuanian culture and mentality' had to be preserved. One interviewee expressed the fear that 'if the Lithuanian birth statistics do not increase, in the next 80 years the Lithuanian nation will be extinct.' Another's fear was that if recent migrants did not get involved in Lithuanian activities, 'the community will disappear.'[31]

About 60 per cent of the interviewees were actively involved in Lithuanian activities – which is not surprising given that they had agreed to take part in a research project investigating Australian Lithuanian national and cultural identity. Some did voluntary work with Saturday school and the Lithuanian press, or involved their children in Lithuanian activities. But for 75 per cent of interviewees, the future of Lithuanian national and cultural activities was bleak. One described the Australian Lithuanian community as 'dying', and warned that unless drastic measures were taken, Lithuanian national and cultural identity would simply fade away. 'We must investigate how Italian, Greek, Jew, Polish or Chinese communities survive', he suggested, 'and how they maintain their identities in Australia.' In his view, a greater development of professional rather than cultural relationships among Lithuanians would have been more useful in creating interest groups and initiating participation in Lithuanian activities through family networks.[32]

For some, organisational change was the key to cultural maintenance. Because there was very little for recent Lithuanian settlers to do in the Lithuanian Houses in Australia, some preferred to visit other clubs, like the Jewish Club in Sydney, which catered for swimmers and had interesting entertainment. Others spent their time at a Polish Club, which had a very good orchestra. Compared with postwar migrants who had lived in Australia for many decades, more recent migrants were still coping with settling-in and were comparatively poor. One regretted that recent migrants, although highly educated, had not been invited to do paid jobs in the Lithuanian Houses, with the result that librarians, musicians, journalists, photographers and teachers sat at home or worked in whatever jobs they could get outside the Lithuanian community. In the meantime, non-professional volunteers staffed Lithuanian schools, libraries, or choirs.[33] It should be noted that postwar

Lithuanian migrants too had the same settling-in problems, but nevertheless spent their time working for the Lithuanian community, with most jobs in the community still voluntary: librarians, Sunday school teachers, folk dance teachers, choir leaders and contributors to Lithuanian periodicals. It should also be noted that quite a few recent arrivals have joined in these activities and have been made to feel welcome.

Individuals make choices for a range of reasons. One respondent commented that she was too busy working full-time to take part in Lithuanian activities. Another lived far away from the Melbourne Lithuanian House, which made it difficult for her and her children to be part of the Lithuanian community. Moreover, she was married to a non-Lithuanian and was more involved in her husband's ethnic community.[34] During her visit to Lithuania in 2002, second wave migrant and professional accordionist gave an interview to the Lithuanian daily *Klaipėda*, outlining how she worked in a factory 12 hours a day, went home, got changed and went to play the accordion at a Chinese restaurant. Initially involved in Lithuanian cultural activities, she soon found herself too busy to dedicate time to the maintenance of her national and cultural identity.[35]

With their first-hand knowledge of the Lithuanian language, recent migrants had had greater scope than afforded to second generation Lithuanian Australians to educate their children in the Lithuanian tradition. But the difficulties associated with finding jobs and settling into their new environment meant many did not have enough time or energy to be involved in Australian Lithuanian activities. It is, then, perhaps not surprising that 20 per cent of the respondents were not convinced that maintaining Lithuanian identity was important.[36]

The question of why some recent migrants do not want to participate in Lithuanian activities in Australia has been raised in the Australian Lithuanian press. Jadvyga Dambrauskienė, an active member of the Australian Lithuanian community, expressed surprise that highly educated recent migrants had not shown greater interest in local Lithuanian activities. 'They rarely come to events organised by postwar Lithuanians', she wrote, regretting that preparing children for the Lithuanian national and cultural activities, or teaching at Saturday school, had become a chore for many. The usual answer was: 'Why me, why do you ask me in particular?'[37] Another commentator, Dr Saulius Varnas, has observed that postwar Lithuanian migrants, who left their country as a consequence of World War II, were not in control of their destinies. In contrast, recent migrants were more flexible in their emigration choices. They were also more preoccupied with their personal lives rather than with involvement in 'old-fashioned Lithuanian ghetto' activities.

Varnas does not agree with the postwar Lithuanian migrant view that the passivity of new arrivals is related to the fact that they were brought up under communism, noting that most descendants of postwar Lithuanian migrants similarly are not part of the Australian Lithuanian community.[38] Varnas is tapping into a deep, emotionally-charged debate within Australia's Lithuanian community. Motives and attitudes are mixed and it is important not to assume a common postwar migrant 'mentality', or discount the very active role that numbers of more recent arrivals do play in Lithuanian community activities. It would be equally misleading to deny the differences between the two groups, or to underestimate the fundamental reassessment and renegotiation of previously fixed views required to reconcile differences. Reconciliation still has some way to go, and the following chapter will explore some of the renegotiation that has occurred as well as some of the differences that still await resolution.

CHAPTER 4

# The changing construction of *lietuvybė* in Australia

## *'Us' and 'them'*

By the 1990s there was a noticeable shift in how Australian Lithuanians viewed events in the homeland and received Lithuanian visitors to Australia's shores. Previously hostile and suspicious of any 'dilution' of 'pure' Lithuanian culture, the demise of Soviet rule made it increasingly untenable for them to reject outright cultural changes in the homeland as necessarily a betrayal of Lithuanian ideals. This reflected the influence of visiting soloists, instrumentalists and dance groups, whose vitality fired the imagination of many – especially younger – Australian Lithuanians. It also reflected the influence of more recent Lithuanian migrants, who, unlike the postwar refugees, were not fleeing persecution and denigration as 'Nazis', 'criminal' or 'undesirable elements'.

Lithuanian migrants who began to arrive in Australia in the 1970s and 1980s did so as the result of Soviet relaxation of control over non-Russian nationalities. True, migration was still a momentous life change, but it did not carry with it the 'do or die' choice that had confronted the postwar refugees. As we saw in Chapter 3, 40 per cent of the later generation of migrants I surveyed and interviewed came to join relatives who had fled the Soviet regime. The research sample was too small to know if they were representative of the entire cohort, but more than half of those surveyed indicated that they had arrived without relatives living in Australia, determined to start a life on their own with greater personal freedom.[1]

Whereas 75 per cent indicated that political reasons were extremely significant or significant motivations for emigration, the figure is only 15 per cent for recent migrants. Similarly, whereas only 10 per cent of the postwar group listed economic reasons as extremely significant or significant, the figure for recent migrants is 25 per cent.[2]

Given the difference in economic motivation, the different employment experiences of the two groups can only be viewed as paradoxical. While many postwar generation Lithuanians had their education cut short and were frustrated by the compulsory two-year contract they had to serve, most completed further education and training in Australia and eventually were able to find employment in their areas of expertise. Although more highly educated and trained on arrival, recently arrived migrants encountered major difficulties in finding employment in their profession and many sought jobs and further training in other areas.

If they were looking for sympathy and help from the older generation of Lithuanians in Australia, some of the newer arrivals would have been disappointed in their early encounters. Some of the postwar generation, who had had no contact with the homeland for 30 years, were suspicious about anyone coming from behind the iron curtain, believing all Lithuanians in the homeland were communists. For their part, some of the new arrivals found it difficult to shake the Soviet attitudes in which they had been schooled, which stereotyped the postwar group as selfish enemies of the state.[3]

The tension between the two groups in those early encounters in the 1970s and 1980s was evident in the interviews I conducted. One postwar generation interviewee remembered well the suspicion towards recent arrivals, who were regarded as 'KGB agents on a mission, secretly spying on us and informing the Soviet authorities on what kind of Lithuanian activities are propagated in Australia.' Overlaying this political suspicion was a widespread view among postwar Lithuanians that the recent arrivals were motivated by materialistic considerations – in contrast to their own pure motivation. 'DPs came here because they were refugees, because they couldn't go back to their homeland,' declared one, 'whereas the immigrants today are economic.'

Another characterised the general view among the postwar generation as 'we are in charge here, we established everything and you just want to reap the benefits of our hard work.' Whereas postwar refugees were united because of their past experiences, recent migrants 'are not interested in *lietuvybė* and only think of how to earn as much money as possible.' For many of the postwar generation who had lived for so many years under the shadow of torture, deportation to Siberia or even death should they ever return to the homeland, the arrival of the new migrants was an unwelcome reminder of the Soviet past.[4]

## *Differences between new arrivals*

A distinction needs to be made between the arrivals of the 1970s and 1980s, coming from Soviet Lithuania, and those of the 1990s, after Lithuania gained its independence. One interviewee recalled how the first new Lithuanian arrivals 'were more modest. They avoided any criticism towards us.' However, the Lithuanians who arrived in the 1990s 'look at us differently, they criticise us, express their views on what we know and forgot. At the same time, we look at them with suspicion, because we notice how 50 years of Soviet occupation affected their thinking.'[5]

Another, who had been told by a recent migrant that nobody gave her a hand when she came, explained that 'obviously they don't seem to feel the need to join the community as such or maybe they are not wanted.' There was an expectation that recent migrants should take part in the Lithuanian activities, but they were here 'for different reasons; they do not want to maintain *lietuvybė*. Instead they wished to settle into their new environment.' With Lithuania now free, one interviewee mused, perhaps recent arrivals saw no reason why *lietuvybė* should be maintained in the diaspora.[6]

Not all members of the postwar generation saw it this way. One suggested that, with many talented young people among the recent arrivals, some members of the postwar generation were motivated by jealousy: 'It's not accepting that Lithuania is free and it's like stopping any opportunity happening too easy, because it was hard for them when they came out, why make it so easy for this new generation?' Another spoke, not in terms of divisions, but of 'a generation gap between older people, born in Lithuania, and young people.' Others agreed that divisions between the different groups might have been due to age, with younger people 'tending to congregate together' through participation in the scouts movement and sports. For one interviewee, there were no divisions between postwar and recent migrants as such – it was more to do with older people being suspicious towards new arrivals. There was, he acknowledged, a lot of criticism towards the new group, 'but looking 50 years back postwar Lithuanians did the same. Their number one priority was to get their family back on their feet, to build the roof over their head. And they did exactly the same as new arrivals are doing now.'[7]

Others agreed that recent migrants were just starting their lives and 'are doing exactly what we did. We wanted to establish ourselves, to buy a house, furniture, a car, everything.' Postwar migrants were already settled, he pointed out, but new arrivals had to take out loans and struggle like every other migrant to this country. One interviewee admitted to feeling broken-hearted about existing divisions: 'There are so few of us in this alien land, so we should not be divided, no matter what our religion and interests are.' Another, in stark contrast, denied any divisions between postwar and recent migrants: 'Every Lithuanian who comes here we meet with love.'[8]

This was not the experience expressed by more than 90 per cent of recently arrived migrants I interviewed. They felt that the Lithuanian community in Australia was divided into groups,[9] one nominating four distinct groups of Australian Lithuanians: the postwar Lithuanians, followed by 'those who have married Australians (mostly for personal gain, rather than for love), economic migrants, and those who emigrated for other motives, such as an unsafe political situation, crime or low morale in Lithuania, inhuman behaviour of individuals, the Australian natural environment.' His experience was that members of the different groups did not like to associate with each other because of their different interests and conflicting life values. Another traced divisions between three main groups: postwar migrants, their descendants, and those who arrived during and after the Soviet era. She considered the most important factor in choosing one's circle of Lithuanian friends was age, followed by education and attitude to traditions. Yet another identified two main groups: Catholics and the rest – the rest being those who practice other religions or who are indifferent to religious beliefs. Within those groups she discerned further differences according to social status, intellect, education, personal interests, sympathies and antipathies.[10]

One interviewee stressed the overriding importance of education as the reason for differences within the community. All of her friends, she explained, studied at university or other tertiary institutions, 'and achieved a very high level of education. By comparison, I have not met many highly educated Lithuanians among those who arrived in Australia after World War II.' Of course, this view privileges a particular understanding of what constitutes a high level of education and, as discussed previously, over 40 per cent of postwar questionnaire respondents had obtained higher level qualifications in Australia, with some 27 per cent completing post-secondary professional qualifications. The same interviewee admitted that she did not like mixing with postwar migrants, which may well account for her not being aware of their achievements. Perhaps she was also missing the intellectual stimulation of being with Lithuanians of her own age and views, as she constantly refers in her interview to the intellectual circles of which she was part in Lithuania.[11]

## *Reasons for suspicion*

Personal views reflect not only one's considered opinion, the 'rational' perspective, but also the 'irrational' impulses, feelings and beliefs that make up one's world-view. One interviewee recalled sharing personal information about her previous employment with a postwar Lithuanian migrant who during a visit to Lithuania was believed to have gone to her previous employer to check whether she really had worked there before coming to Australia. The interviewee regarded this as an insult and as a result wanted no further involvement with the Lithuanian community.[12]

Hers is not an isolated experience. Another interviewee complained about postwar migrants' attitudes towards new migrants, recalling an incident the day he arrived in Australia, when he took his whole family to Melbourne Lithuanian House. He wanted to meet local Lithuanians and inquire about life in a new country. At the door he was greeted with the insult: 'Lithuania is free now. Why then are you coming here – for better economic advantages? Go back to where you belong.' His comeback was that some Lithuanians had settled in Australia after World War I, others after World War II, others were arriving now and would continue to arrive in the future: 'there is nothing postwar migrants can do to stop us!' As a result of the 'welcome', neither he nor his family had any intention of returning to Lithuanian House or of becoming involved in the community.[13]

Others confirmed that Lithuanian House was not always a welcoming place: 'Postwar migrants never notice or talk to you; even if you stay at the front door for an hour, nobody would come and have a sincere conversation with you.'[14] There were complaints that the fact that postwar Lithuanians had lived here for a long time had made them superior to recent migrants: trying to teach them how to do things 'the right way' and rejecting out of hand new ideas coming from recent arrivals. Many would have liked to take part in Lithuanian activities, but were simply not invited. A university graduate from Lithuania recalls how she was too shy to come forward. 'How should I do it? Why do postwar migrants not invite recent migrants? However, when recent migrants show some initiative, they are criticised.'[15]

One recent arrival spoke of the divisions he perceived between the first and subsequent generations of the postwar cohort. In his view, the main dividing line was based on age and the use of the Lithuanian language for communication. 'The young generation that has grown up in Australia keeps away from the old generation', he observed. 'The overwhelming majority of them communicates almost exclusively in English and seldom participates in the community activities of the older generation. The older members of the community themselves are divided between those who are close to the Catholic Church and people with more liberal views.' He went on to surmise that, due to their war trauma, some postwar Lithuanians hold unrealistic ambitions. In marked contrast, another recent arrival was blissfully unaware of *any* groupings within the Lithuanian community because he and his family members did not mix with Lithuanians, preferring to create a circle of friends, who were not necessarily Lithuanian. 'In Australia, as in Lithuania', he stressed, 'we associate with people of similar intellect and interests' – the implied value judgement being that postwar migrants were poorly educated and of a lower intelligence than the more recent arrivals.[16] This was an unfair stereotype, but there is no denying such projections played a part in the decisions of some recent arrivals to repudiate connection with the community.

Among the postwar questionnaire respondents, more than 45 per cent considered their relationship with recently arrived Lithuanians to be excellent or good, with the same percentage judging it to be just satisfactory or poor. According to one interviewee, in the eyes of postwar migrants everything associated with Russian influence was regarded with great suspicion. For instance, Lithuanian songs that had incorporated party slogans such as the 'Lenin genius' or the 'Strength of Soviet Union' – which during the Soviet era had come to be hardly noticed by people in Lithuania – were vehemently rejected in Australia, and if such songs were chosen for performance by Australian Lithuanians the offending words were replaced by neutral expressions. Not having been resocialised in the same way as Lithuanians in Soviet Lithuania, postwar Australian Lithuanians remained highly sensitive to such influences. Another recalled how, in the early 1970s, when a Russian group arrived in Australia for concerts, local Lithuanians, especially of the older generation, were frightened of the group because they associated Russians with communism. 'They can't forget it, it's just something almost like engraved, the hatred of communism. Of course, Russians automatically become communists.' Another confirmed that even the famous Lithuanian opera soloist Virgilijus Noreika received a cold reception at his 1981 performance because he was a suspect in the eyes of the postwar Lithuanian migrants.[17]

## *Fractured relationships*

It was a common view that the postwar arrivals were DPs who could not return to Lithuania, whereas the motives of more recent migrants were more economic. This was seen by some as the main reason for the tensions between the two groups. 'Postwar migrants were trying to work together, because they needed an identity, they needed that security of their own group', one of the postwar generation explained. 'I don't think that new migrants need it as much as then, as it was needed in those days.' Another expressed how recent migrants with few exceptions were viewed as materialistic, as a consequence of the Soviet inheritance. 'People have changed, with so much bureaucracy in Lithuania, where the ordinary secretary could order you around as much as she feels like.' She explained that as postwar migrants had escaped with the fear of being deported to Siberia, they clung to a nostalgia for the past. In contrast, recent migrants did not even know what nostalgia was: 'I have asked a lady from Lithuania whether she feels nostalgic for her homeland, and she asked me what does it mean!' Another member of the postwar generation noted how, on her return to Lithuania, she was not even able to communicate with her sisters. 'Their problems are so different to mine.' People in Lithuania, she felt, had very low morals – the whole system having been exposed to corruption. Another found it surprising that elderly people in Lithuania still praised the Soviet system, stating that they had a much better life before independence, which she concluded was evidence that people had been 'brainwashed by Russians.'[18]

Overall, 45 per cent of postwar group respondents considered their relationship with recent arrivals as excellent or good. In contrast, only 20 per cent of recent migrant respondents viewed their relationship with postwar group as excellent or good. Recent migrants had come to Australia 'with open hearts' one proffered, but were met 'with uncertainty, with a desire to investigate our past.' This same person described the intellect of many postwar migrants as very limited, and claimed there was not much in common between the two groups. Here again we see the projection of stereotypes, which tends to become a self-fulfilling prophecy in terms of interaction between the two groups. Postwar Lithuanian migrants did not have a healthy relationship amongst themselves, complained another recent arrival, so how could they be expected to get along with recent migrants? Another took issue with postwar migrants calling themselves exiles: 'What kind of exiles are they, safely hidden in Australia, with their brothers and sisters being tortured by the Soviet apparatchiks or killed in Siberia?'[19]

## *Contested identities*

Among the recently arrived migrants I interviewed, were people who had experienced psychological trauma in Lithuania. One described how she had been expelled from the Pedagogical Institute when KGB agents discovered that her father, a military officer, had been sent to Siberia. In her application for tertiary studies she had written that her father had passed away, but KGB agents had uncovered his whereabouts and she was forced to leave her studies. 'I will never forget my struggles and the tragedy that my father was taken away from me.' Another's husband had been expelled from the Polytechnic Institute because KGB agents discovered that his father, a 'bourgeois element', was living in Australia. She added that her father-in-law had been sent to Queensland for his two-year contract to work on sugar plantations where he was 'fed and looked after' by the Australian government. In contrast, his wife and son were exposed to Soviet persecution because he had run away from the Soviet Union.[20]

Another recent migrant interviewee found that postwar Lithuanian migrants did not like what they called the Russianised language they had learnt in Soviet Lithuania, which made communication between them difficult. One would go to a cricket match, with which she had no cultural connection or familiarity, rather than Lithuanian House for 'old-fashioned entertainment.' Another described how whatever she did in the presence of postwar migrants was never good enough: 'Oh, you dress so differently, you do this and that, not the way we are used to do here.' While she felt that she was treated 'a little bit better' than other recent migrants because she was married to a postwar Lithuanian migrant, she was still uncomfortable with her life being 'placed under the microscope.' 'You are from the Soviet Union', she was reminded, 'therefore how can you understand chemistry, medicine? How do you know how to drive a car? What do you know about anything, you are from the Soviet Union!' More highly educated Lithuanians of the postwar cohort, she found, were more tolerant and understanding, while the less educated were more dogmatic and dictatorial.[21]

The divisions between the groups were frequently discussed in the local Lithuanian press. A prominent postwar Australian Lithuanian Gabrielius Žemkalnis noted that recent migrants with a practical profession like accountancy or computer programming and a good knowledge of English were able to settle into their new environment with relative ease, whereas others lived a constant struggle. Previous social status became irrelevant. Some had left Lithuania with a romanticised image of life abroad, believing that 'the money grows on trees, people live happily, without any troubles or concerns, and achieved everything without hard work.' Žemkalnis recalled unpleasant confrontations with new arrivals, whose only desire was to get rich quickly. In his opinion the general attitude of postwar Lithuanian migrants towards them was warm. What was necessary was for new arrivals to get involved in Lithuanian community activities on a voluntary basis[22] – a view that mirrors that of many of the postwar participants' I surveyed in the course of my research.

Some recently arrived Lithuanians did become closely involved in local community activities. Dalia Didžienė, Lilija Kozlovskienė, Jadvyga Dambrauskienė, Dalia Doniela and Saulius Varnas are all well known in the social circles of the postwar group because of their community involvement. Other recent arrivals I interviewed had worked in different Lithuanian committees, or the Lithuanian press, or been involved in planning for Australian Lithuanian Days (ALDs). Others involved their children and grandchildren in Lithuanian activities.

Recent migrant Petras Vegys expressed concern that the number of Sydney Lithuanian Club members was dwindling thus bringing the financial sustainability of the Club under question. Attracting more recent arrivals into postwar Lithuanian migrants' activities was seen as the way forward, but the Club kept coming up against the deep cultural divide between the two groups. As Vegys noted, postwar Lithuanian migrants created Lithuanian organisations in Australia in order to compensate for the loss of the homeland and to keep their spirits high by maintaining Lithuanian national and cultural activities in the diaspora. The Lithuanian Club was not only the place where Lithuanian identity could be maintained, but also the place where displaced Lithuanian nationals could feel at home. In contrast to the fundamental displacement experienced by postwar migrants, most recent Lithuanian migrants came to Australia primarily to work and create wealth, leaving their families behind. They did not treat the Lithuanian Club as their home because, in Vegys's view, they had not cut their ties with their homeland and their loved ones, and therefore did not have the same need to participate in local Lithuanian national and cultural activities. The simple reason that the Sydney Lithuanian Club was unable to attract recently arrived Lithuanians – or the descendants of postwar migrants – according to Vegys, was that they felt there was 'nothing to do at the Club. In comparison to postwar migrants they have a quite different relationship with a Club.' The most the Sydney Lithuanian Club could offer them was a cheap beer and a game of pool. [23]

Another recently arrived Lithuanian, Janina Malijauskienė, expanded on Vegys's observation, writing that tensions between postwar and recent migrants reflected a generational gap and different attitudes towards identity. While the preservation of Lithuanian culture away from home was a matter of great importance, it was also important to stop lingering on past experiences and work towards creating a strong and stable cultural base relevant to the new context. If they were not to disappear into the wider community, Lithuanians had to move away from their distant past. This included postwar migrants who had lived away from their homeland for decades and who had renegotiated their language skills during that time. They had to cease blaming new arrivals for the 'distortion' of the Lithuanian language by 'Russianisation' which they sometimes found difficult to understand. Similarly, there had to be greater tolerance for the cultural changes brought to Australia by recently arrived Lithuanians, and an acceptance by postwar migrants that recent migrants who had grown up with different life values did not have to think 'like us'.[24]

The month following Malijauskienė's comments, postwar migrant Dr Algimantas Kabaila made a speech at the Australian Lithuanian Council's (ALDs) Convention in Sydney which sparked a wave of controversy when it was published in the Australian Lithuanian weekly *Mūsų Pastogė*

(Our Heaven). Kabaila argued that communist ideology had influenced Lithuanians in the homeland to believe that postwar Lithuanian migrants had fled the country simply looking for a better life. One must never forget, he stressed, the communist occupation of the Lithuanian soil and the sufferings of millions of innocent citizens: 'We must constantly remind the world of the outcome of communism.' Kabaila's view was that a relationship between postwar Lithuanian migrants and new arrivals was not possible unless recent migrants condemned communism and got involved as volunteers in the Lithuanian community in Australia. Rita Baltušytė, editor of *Mūsų Pastogė* at the time, had no doubt that new arrivals would voluntarily contribute to the Lithuanian community in Australia, but she questioned Kabaila's requirement for new arrivals to condemn communism. 'How in particular can one condemn it?' In a later contribution Kabaila claimed that Baltušytė had misunderstood his speech at the ALC convention. But he went further, accusing the editor of 'typical Soviet style journalism.'[25]

The debate not only illustrates the at times strained relationship between postwar and recent migrants, but also points to the challenges faced by Lithuanian migrants at *any* time in renegotiating their cultural relationships within and beyond the Lithuanian community. Identity in Australia is a complex matter, with a multiplicity of identities positioned between and among different groups of Lithuanians. Some postwar Lithuanian migrants might have enjoyed the company of other nationals who came to Australia on the same ship, or lived in the same village. Similarly, migrants who settled in Australia during the years of Soviet occupation shared different common experiences. Those who emigrated in the 1990s, after Lithuania became independent, share different experiences again. It is understandable that the different groups would have had quite different ideas about how *lietuvybė* should or should not be maintained in Australia.

This echoes historian Ieva Zake's investigation of the relationship between the different groups of American-Latvians who settled in America after World War I, after World War II, and those who were born in America. Zake found the main reasons why people of the same nationality may not get along depended on their political and historical views towards their homeland and their homeland citizens' perceptions towards them.[26] The relationship between Australian Lithuanians of the postwar generation and their homeland was strained. On the one hand, they were born and bred in Lithuania, and lost their land, houses and possessions due to the war. On the other hand, because they ran away from the dangers of war and were saved from being killed or deported, in the eyes of Soviet authorities they were regarded as traitors of the state. On their visits to Lithuania, postwar generation migrants were often viewed simply as visitors by their family members and friends. Due to the physical and psychological separation that resulted from the splitting the Lithuanian nation, even members of the same family were unable to find common ground after independence.

Different life experiences impact on personal and group identity. Identity is not a fixed and immutable state of being. As Avtar Brah has written:

> The idea of identity, like that of culture, is singularly elusive. We speak of 'this' identity and 'that' identity. We know from our everyday experience that what we call 'me' or 'I' is not the same in every situation; that we are changing from day to day. Yet there is something we 'recognise' in ourselves and in others which we call 'me' and 'you' and 'them'. In other words, we are all constantly changing but this *changing illusion* is precisely what we *see* as real and concrete about ourselves and others. And this *seeing* is both a social and a psychological process. Identity then is an enigma which, by its very nature, defies a precise definition.[27]

As Brah notes, the reason that people recognise a common identity is that they have lived through similar experiences: postwar migrants distinctly identified themselves as DPs; recent migrants who arrived in Australia before and after Lithuania regained its independence identified themselves as Soviet or post-Soviet citizens. The common experience of arriving on the same ship, of living behind the iron curtain, or in free country after the 1990s, could give rise to very different senses of identity.

## *Future of* lietuvybė

As discussed in Chapter 2, postwar Lithuanian nationals were locked into the view that the only way to save their national identity was to *preserve* it in Australia through their voluntary activities. They expected recent migrants to continue the traditional voluntary work within the Lithuanian community, as an important element in their understanding of what it was to be Lithuanian was to make a contribution to the community. Recently arrived Lithuanians had a different understanding of what *lietuvybė* in Australia means. One interviewee made the point that the Soviet occupation tried to create a new type of individual, Homo Sovieticus. In Lithuania people encountered widespread aggression, brutality, malicious acts, and suppression of personal freedom. During the Soviet period, the people of Lithuania were obliged to conform and blend into one big family, where personality was suppressed and individual intellectual voices silenced. Those who tried to move against the tide were persecuted or rejected by other members of society. Superficially, this would seem to support the myth created by members of the postwar Lithuanian generation that *lietuvybė* could only survive outside of Soviet Lithuania in an enclosed community, detached from the mainstream. But as the recent arrival who referred to Homo Sovieticus explained, the 'underground identity survived in Lithuania as well.'[28]

Interviews with other recent Lithuanian migrants confirmed that some had problems 'fitting into' postwar groups' activities. Some explained that they did not get involved in Lithuanian activities because from the time of their arrival they were faced with such attitudes as: 'You came here on your own accord and now we'll see how you can establish yourself without our help.' Others believed that postwar Lithuanian migrants in Australia held onto a prewar identity, which was why new migrants were unable to relate to their activities. They also noted that the Lithuanian language of postwar generation was old-fashioned and had failed to adjust to changed circumstances. Within their enclosed community, postwar migrants tried to protect themselves from non-postwar and foreign influences and were missing out on the opportunity to capitalise on the professional expertise of recent migrants or non-Lithuanians to revitalise the community.[29]

Of the 32 Australian-born people of Lithuanian descent I surveyed, almost 90 per cent believed that the maintenance of Lithuanian national and cultural identity was important. What they meant by important was elaborated in the 17 interviews. One interviewee was certain that '*lietuvybė* will never die in Melbourne, in Australia, or in other countries as long as there were people who are prepared to do the work.' He pointed out that while Lithuanians may marry non-Lithuanians, they continue to stay enthusiastic about their ancestral land. 'Lithuanian people are very social and that's why the candle will still burn whether it's a [flicker] or it's a flame.' He recalled that in the past older Lithuanians rejected the participation of younger Lithuanians in various councils. What was needed was for the young people to stand up and take control, otherwise the community would not stay alive or Lithuanian House survive. 'It's really important to have a central focus, somewhere where people gather together [even] if they gather once a year, with someone that they know.'[30]

Another interviewee suggested that Lithuanian singing, dancing, scouting and sports activities had to continue, even if the dwindling number of Lithuanian participants was replaced with Australians. One gave the example of the Lithuanian dance group in Tasmania, which had three Australian-born Lithuanians, with many others who 'had nothing to do with Lithuania. But they were interested in being part of the cultural dance group.' Similarly, the Adelaide Lithuanian dance group was always looking 'for anyone who is willing to dance.' 'Whether the Lithuanian culture continues as purely Lithuanian or whether we all mix outside with other Australians', one interviewee observed, 'we're still interested in keeping up and being Lithuanian in some way!' By exposing Lithuanian identity to the mainstream, these descendants were indicating that they themselves felt part of it.[31]

Other members of the younger generation expressed a sense of exclusion from the Lithuanian community. One complained that postwar Lithuanians did not wish to sing the songs of other nationalities and stuck to the music of Lithuanian composers. That was why they 'haven't been able to change, to keep up, keep a sense of relevance. That isolates a lot of people. Excludes them.' Another felt equally discouraged:

> I worked in the community a lot with a Sports Club. We were and are trying our best when we do lunches as similar as possible to what the older generation did, but it's never gonna be the same because we haven't had the same upbringing and all you get back is negative, and it ends up at the stage, well, why should we bother then to try to please you? Why should we bother carrying on any traditions if it's not acceptable?

At the same time, postwar migrants would not let recent migrants participate in the community's life, because 'they wish to keep going to the day they die and then they complain where is the community?'[32]

The maintenance of Lithuanian national and cultural identity in Australia depends on the willingness of descendants to get involved in future activities. The number of Lithuanian-born people in Australia is decreasing. According to the Australian Bureau of Statistics, in 2006 only 2,005 people who spoke Lithuanian at home. By 2011 this number had dropped to 1,899. With decreasing numbers of Lithuanian-born migrants in Australia, and the postwar generation dying out, it is the descendants of postwar migrants who will be the future leaders. Some do not wish to be involved or feel excluded from postwar migrants' activities and prefer to become part of the mainstream. Constant comparisons between us (descendants) and them (postwar migrants) or between us (postwar migrants) and them (recent arrivals) keep the different generations apart. The future of *lietuvybė* lies with the younger generations of Australian-born Lithuanians, and inevitably their activities will be hybridised.

Views on *lietuvybė*, or being Lithuanian in a non-Lithuanian setting, are changing in line with the constant renegotiation of the relationship between the homeland and the diaspora. The connection between diasporic communities and the homeland does not have to disappear. On the contrary, while being absorbed into different national and cultural identities,

Lithuanians have the opportunity to keep their constantly evolving links with the homeland alive. Although *lietuvybė* is important to both postwar and recent migrants, the first group has tended to preserve their identity by gathering in the Lithuanian Clubs and Houses and continuing the national and cultural activities they initiated more than half a century ago. By contrast, recent Lithuanian migrants have reasons to escape from their Soviet past and seek personal independence and freedom in their new country.

The relationship between and among different groups of Lithuanians in Australia is not a straightforward matter that can be resolved simply by inviting recently arrived Lithuanians to join in existing activities, or by establishing an information centre to assist recent migrants on arrival and make them welcome in the Lithuanian community. The reality is more complex, experiences more differentiated, to be accommodated by simple 'solutions'. The future of the Australian Lithuanian community will depend on the extent to which Lithuanians wish to be in touch with *lietuvybė* – especially through the Lithuanian language and singing – and in the following chapter we will consider the influence of other cultures on the survival of the Lithuanian language and singing in the diaspora.

Adelaide Baltic singers commemorating deportations, n.y.

Demonstration of three Baltic states, Adelaide, 1989

Canberra Lithuanians, 1950

Canberra Lithuanian choir, 1968

Canberra Lithuanians, 1981

Geelong Lithuanian Šatrija scout troops, 1963

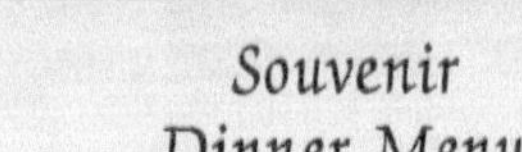

Souvenir
Dinner Menu

24th January 1998
Laetare Gardens

**Above**

Geelong Lithuanian celebrations in honour of Saint Kazimier, 1980

**Left**

50 years Baltic migrants, Hobart, 1998

Hobart Lithuanian commemoration of deportations, 2006

Melbourne Lithuanians, 1960s–70s

Melbourne Lithuanians, 1970s

Melbourne Lithuanian folk ensemble Pamesta klumpė (Lost clog), 2014

Sydney Lithuanian group Šviesa (The Light), 1954

Sydney Lithuanian students at Bateau Bay, 1960

Sydney Lithuanian Press festival, 2001

Perth Lithuanians with Bishop Vincentas Brizgys, 1965

Combined Geelong and Melbourne Lithuanian girl guide troops, Victoria, 1972

Combined Australian Lithuanian song and dance group, Melbourne, 1994

Combined Australian Lithuanian performers, Trakai, Lithuania, 1994

Australian Lithuanian Song Festival, Melbourne, 2010

CHAPTER 5

# The construction of 'Lithuania' in Australia through language and singing

## *Linguistic misunderstandings*

Detached from the homeland and introduced into a new environment, any language is exposed to great challenges. As part of the process of blending into the host society, the use by migrants of the host language is largely unavoidable. Even a language like Lithuanian, which had successfully resisted formidable challenges to its survival in the past, is threatened during this process. Developed from 'the most archaic' Indo-European languages[1] in about the fourth and third centuries BC, around the eighth century AD Lithuanian was separated from the Latvian language, which underwent modernisation and simplification of grammar and form. While other Indo-European languages underwent transformations, the Lithuanian language remained relatively unchanged. It retained many of its original morphologies, archaic sound systems and lexical features, leading Theodore S. Thurston to conclude: 'The vowel system of the Lithuanian language is the most ancient in its style. It pre-dates Sanskrit, Latvian, Greek and Latin, in that order.'[2]

At the same time as linguists like Thurston were marvelling at the survival of an ancient language like Lithuanian, officials in Australia were keen to get migrants' English skills up to speed. In postwar Australia, languages like Lithuanian were perceived as part of a problem. Teaching English to 'New

Australians' English is difficult, Esmond Barclay observed, 'not because they don't want to learn English, but because they are such an immense variety of people ... Each nation has its own phonetics; some don't even use our alphabet.' According to Barclay, education officers 'estimated that 70,000 of those who studied under the scheme speak fairly good English. Another 50,000 are making good progress ... However, 50,000 still need tuition.' Barclay pointed out that only 10,000 to 11,000 regularly attended English classes. This would have disappointed the Immigration Department, which was contributing £150,000 to £200,000 a year to migrant tuition, in order to teach New Australians to speak like 'real Australians'.[3]

Through the Australian Broadcasting Commission's radio programs, migrants had free access to English lessons twice a week. Extracts from these ABC lessons were available in Lithuanian community newspapers, to help those struggling with conversational English. For newcomers, the 'lack of English was most embarrassing ...' When a man asked a shopkeeper for 'tuzen aks', he was given a dozen axes, not eggs.[4] Government policy was reinforced by the perceptions within the general public, with Lithuanians speaking among themselves in the Lithuanian language being interrupted by Anglo-Celtic Australians, who would complain: 'You are in Australia now, speak English.'[5] The government's concern that 'DPs are learning English with difficulty'[6] implied that they did not have an ability to learn. The reality that postwar Lithuanians, like other migrants, came to Australia mostly as adults and, instead of studying English, had to work long and hard to support their families, seems to have been lost on policy-makers as much as the wider population.

What also went unrecognised was that most Lithuanians wanted to retain their mother tongue. Today, in a multicultural environment, such a desire needs no apology or further explanation. As Jacques Derrida has commented:

> The language of the immigrants ... should be kept alive, allowed to feed into and disturb the dominant tongue, in order to preserve these rich national differences and ancient

memories, and also to keep the experience of speaking and thinking *otherwise* alive.[7]

## Maintaining 'pure' language

Their number is shrinking, but after more than half a century of living in Australia the first wave Lithuanian migrants still keep close to their original language, and maintain the dialect brought from their place of birth. Struggling to support themselves and their families in the often culturally hostile environment of postwar Australia, they nevertheless initiated the Lithuanian Cultural Foundation as early as 1948, and encouraged the creation of Lithuanian Saturday schools to keep the language alive for their children. The schools were founded in Adelaide in 1949, Melbourne 1950, Bankstown and Geelong 1951, and Canberra 1952. However, the postwar generation children's ability to communicate in Lithuanian was destabilised by the pressure to speak English at home. As linguistic researcher Michael Clyne confirmed, during the heyday of assimilation, 'Many teachers advised parents to use nothing but English at home, regardless of how badly they spoke it.'[8]

While Lithuanian parents were encouraging their children to attend Lithuanian Saturday schools, their children were not only speaking more and more English, but were also being made to feel ashamed or inferior when they did use Lithuanian. In postwar Australia, migrants who persisted in speaking their first language, especially in public or to their children, were regarded as unAustralian. Postwar Lithuanian children were made to feel different from other Australian students, not only because of their language, but also because of their cultural perceptions. A postwar Lithuanian migrant recalled how Anglo-Celtic Australian children would laugh at Lithuanians who spoke amongst each other in their own language. He tells a story of how a 13-year-old girl, who came to school from a rural village and spoke only Lithuanian, was verbally abused not only by other children, but even by her teacher.[9] Like other 'ethnic' children, Lithuanian children were subjected to taunts and classroom discrimination in ways that would today be illegal.

Many Australian parents 'did not want their children to be in classes with migrants', Peter Musgrave observed at the time.[10] Migrant children were pressured to blend in with the rest and to speak English. Lithuanian children, because of their 'Anglo-Saxon' looks and ability to adapt quickly, were saved from further humiliation. But these same 'qualities' also served to further undermine their interest in maintaining their parents' language.

There were some promising signs. In 1975, the Lithuanian language was introduced at Matriculation level in schools, and minority language courses were funded by state and federal governments. Examination bodies for High School Certificate Lithuanian were established in Victoria in the same year, in South Australia in 1978, and in New South Wales in 1980.[11] The 1978 Galbally Strategy for migrant settlement recommended teaching migrant languages in schools and promoting multicultural education in order to impact upon school curricula, and, in 1984, a Senate Committee recognised the importance of second-language learning in schools. It was uncertain how far bilingual education should be recommended, and government departments and agencies were cautious in their support for the programs. The Schools Commission stressed these programs should be transitional and dismissed the possibility of bilingual maintenance programs. The Senate Committee found that while 60 per cent of Year 7 students studied languages, this reduced to 12 per cent by Year 12. Despite teachers being encouraged to teach 'as many languages as possible ...',[12] the eminent multicultural advocate Jerzy Smolicz considered that the multicultural education introduced in a number of schools was a complete waste of time and resources. This was partially the outcome of the 1950s assimilation policy that encouraged migrants to speak English only.[13]

In the meantime, Lithuanian children continued with their ethnic schooling on weekends. But as postwar Lithuanian descendant observed, it became 'almost impossible if the parents speak no Lithuanian but expect their children to learn the language from a two and a half hour a week lesson at Lithuanian school.'[14] Children from mixed marriages in particular experienced difficulties in learning Lithuanian. Inevitably, the younger generation did not have the same determination as their parents to preserve

Lithuanian, which increasingly found its expression as a recreated and reinvented language suspended between two socio-linguistic poles.

The loss was acknowledged by Governor-General Sir Ninian Stephen in his address to the nation on Australia Day 1989:

> The thing that distresses me is how little most children and grandchildren of overseas-born Australians seem to be retaining of the culture and especially of the language of their lands of origin ... We should be a nation of great linguists ... Yet 30 years down the track, with a new, Australian-born generation, that mother tongue so often is lost forever.[15]

Since then, due to the shrinking Lithuanian community and changed priorities at Australian universities, community language courses have come under renewed threat, with Lithuanian becoming one of the 'low-demand' courses within university programs.[16]

## *Preservation of traditions*

For third generation Australian Lithuanians, born and educated in Australia, identifying as Lithuanian does not entail the same attachment to the language that their parents and – more especially – their grandparents had. National celebrations such as Lithuanian Independence Day and the commemoration of Exiled to Siberia Day hold little meaning for a generation that has not experienced the horrors of war, or the fear of being sent to Siberia. While they continue to dance Lithuanian national dances and sing in folklore groups, this is no longer experienced as a means of preserving a separate Lithuanian identity, and if Australian-born Lithuanians invite non-Lithuanians to participate in their cultural activities it is to spend more time with their friends. This is anathema to some elderly Lithuanians who perceive such cultural mixing as a threat to their national survival. However, from the perspective of third generation Australian Lithuanians, sharing their Lithuanian heritage with their non-Lithuanian friends can be seen as a natural and legitimate expression of Lithuanian identity.

In the late 1990s, the Melbourne Lithuanian community activist Dalia Didžienė commented on the third generation's continuing interest in Lithuanian activities. The experiential basis had shifted, with significant implications for language maintenance. When the Melbourne Lithuanian dance group Gintaras (Amber) participated in the World Lithuanian Dance Festival in Lithuania in 1994, the young dancers showed initiative by learning some Lithuanian in order to communicate with people in Lithuania, but found it much easier to speak to each other in English.[17] I coordinated and conducted the combined Australian Lithuanian choir in Lithuania in 1994 and was acutely aware that, with their limited Lithuanian vocabulary, the Australian-born Lithuanian singers could not be expected to have had their parents' and grandparents' understanding of the meaning of the words they were singing. The Lithuanian songs sung at these concerts were mostly sentimental and sad, reflecting on the years of living in separation from the homeland, but the young singers found it difficult to sustain a serious expression, because the words did not reflect a first-hand experience. In contrast with their neutral expressions, the elderly Australian Lithuanian singers, who understood and experienced the significance of the songs, looked genuinely sad and tearful. Singing 'Waltzing Matilda', the youth were full of energy, but most of the elderly Lithuanians seemed ill at ease struggling with the English pronunciation. As Lithuanian newspapers remarked at the time, the young Lithuanians from Australia spoke English and experienced the Lithuanian language as a distant exotic trace of their parents' traditional past.

## *Implications of multilingualism*

Changes to the traditional past can be traced back to 1947, when Lithuanian refugees first set foot on Australian soil and were obliged to accommodate to the new setting, including the linguistic environment. The practice of adding the Lithuanian suffixes *as* or *is* to English words effectively created a new vocabulary. Thus the English word pub became *pabas*, replacing the Lithuanian word *aludė*. *Niursė* (nurse) replaced *seselė*, *bosas* (boss) *viršininkas*, *karpenteris* (carpenter) *stalius*, *butčeris* (butcher) *mėsininkas*, and so on. These changes bear out linguist Einar Haugen's observation that language competence 'is a skill with a market value that determines who will acquire it ... Even ... the first language we learn ... will be maintained only if it serves as a medium of communication with speakers with whom we wish to communicate.'[18]

When I distributed a bilingual questionnaire as part of my research in 1999–2000, 20 per cent of participants replied to the English version. Of the 80 per cent of respondents who replied to the Lithuanian language questionnaire in Lithuanian, 10 per cent used a combination of Lithuanian and English while 5 per cent chose to answer the Lithuanian questionnaire in English. Although the English questionnaire targeted descendants of postwar Lithuanian migrants, some postwar migrants themselves found it more useful than the Lithuanian. During interviews with this group, all 42 interviewees used a combination of Lithuanian and English. If one respondent in a focus group of two and three chose to speak English, others immediately switched to English. English words such as dentistry, chemistry, hospital, high school, college and labourer were used by interviewees who otherwise spoke Lithuanian. At the same time, interviewees talking in English inserted Lithuanian words such as *skautai* (scouts) and *paskaitos* (lectures) into their conversation. There were also many examples of linguistic mixture or creolisation in the interviews, such as *hotelis* (hotel), *biskvitas* (biscuit), *aksidentas* (accident) or *multikultūrinis* (multicultural).[19]

There are numerous examples of bilingualism in the Australian Lithuanian press. Although an article by Paulius Kviecinskas has a Lithuanian title: 'Melbourno "Džiugo" tunto stovykla' ('Džiugas' tuntas' scout camp in Melbourne), it is written in English. Many Lithuanian words in the article, such as *stovykla* (camp), *draugystė* (friendship), *Užgavėnės* (Shrovetide) and *adjutantas* (aide de camp), have been inserted into the English text without translation.[20] The article, with the main scout expressions untranslated, demonstrates not only how postwar Lithuanians pass Lithuanian scouting traditions onto their descendants, but also how many elements of the Lithuanian national and cultural identity remain strong. In another article,

Alė Liubinienė describes a journey to an exotic island. In order to ensure that readers of the Australian Lithuanian newspaper *Tėviškės Aidai* (The Homeland Echoes) understand the meaning of her words, Liubinienė titles her article in English, followed by a translation into Lithuanian: 'Easter Island (Velykų sala).' Although writing in Lithuanian, she translates some words into English, and puts them in parenthesis, for example, *tuštumoje* (blowhole). At the same time, Liubinienė chooses not to offer translation of the English words disco, souvenirs, No … No … Five dollars, or prime minister.[21]

Whether they choose to be a part of the Australian Lithuanian community or not, adapting to their new environment necessarily entails Lithuanian migrants' use of the English language. Among recently arrived migrants, knowledge of English varies considerably. Three quarters of respondents assessed themselves as having only a satisfactory or poor command of English. Approximately 10 per cent used some English words in their Lithuanian questionnaire.

Interviews with this group confirmed that all attempted to speak English, though 20 per cent experienced difficulties in writing in English and 20 per cent in reading in English. At the same time, English has impacted on their Lithuanian usage. For example, one interviewee used the expression 'pirmas dalykas' (first thing), which in Lithuanian would correctly be 'pirmiausiai' (first of all). Sentence structure was also affected: 'Atvykus, Australijoje septynis metus nedirbau niekur' (After arrival in Australia, I did not work for seven years), which should be 'Atvykus į Australiją, septynis metus niekur nedirbau.'[22] What may be concluded from these examples is that even where Lithuanian is used in Australia it has been exposed to English influences, and in terms of formal grammar has suffered as a consequence.

Only 10 per cent of the group used other languages. Knowledge of Russian – the second language of most Lithuanians growing up in the Soviet system – is not of much use in Australia. Not only did the majority of recent Lithuanian migrants learn the Russian language at school, but they were also exposed to Russian influences in everyday living. Sales persons, train conductors, and army officers who settled in Lithuania from other Russian-speaking countries of the Soviet Union often spoke only Russian, and Lithuanians who travelled within the Soviet Union found themselves most of the time conversing in Russian. My own experience while living in Lithuania is typical: I had to speak Russian to my Estonian friend, because it was our only common language. Today we correspond in English, as a matter of choice.[23] Each day in Australia members of the Lithuanian community make similar choices. Some strive to remain multilingual, using Lithuanian, Russian and English. Others are determined to remain (or become) bilingual, using Lithuanian and English. Others have shifted to English alone.

This switching between languages has major implications for the future of Lithuanian identity in Australia. To the question 'What aspects of Lithuanian culture are you most attached to?' 65 per cent of respondents replied 'the Lithuanian language', and for 80 per cent of recently arrived Lithuanians the main language they used at home was Lithuanian. While the majority speak Lithuanian as their language of choice, during interviews some inserted English terms, such as 'Australijoje baigiau Australijos Medical Council egzaminus' (I have completed the Australian Medical Council Examinations in Australia). The combination of Lithuanian and English is an example of linguistic and cultural hybridisation to relate the conversation to the new environment. Such hybridisation is unavoidable given that some English words and cultural expressions are untranslatable. This might be a cause of regret for some in terms of formal linguistics, but in terms of maintaining competence in their use of Lithuanian and at the same time improving their English, such practices can be viewed as evidence of how these migrants have become linguistically and culturally diverse and adaptive.[24]

Linguistic hybridisation is not confined to the diaspora. One postwar generation interviewee described how upon her return to Lithuania she often found it difficult to understand the Lithuanian language in print, with people's surnames greatly distorted.[25] In the daily press former US President Bill Clinton became *Bilas Klintonas,* and well-known Australian actress Nicole Kidman *Nikolė Kidmanė*. Computer language is similarly hybridised, with computer rendered *kompiuteris*, printer *printeris*, and scanner *skeneris*.

Such changes 'back home', have only reinforced the view of some postwar Lithuanians that they are the custodians of linguistic and national 'purity'. As one interviewee explained, 'In Australia we were able to preserve our pure language. Unfortunately now the language and other human qualities in the homeland are not the same.' Another acknowledged that although they left the homeland a long time ago, 'we still live in a prewar Lithuania and remember it the way we left it.' For many, they were responsible for the 'preservation of Lithuanian national and cultural identity in the diaspora during the years of the Soviet occupation of Lithuania.'[26] This helps explain postwar Lithuanian researcher Algimantas Taškūnas' preoccupation with what he considers the unnecessary use of Anglicised words, and his attempt to decreolise the Lithuanian language in his 1998 book *Nereikalingų svetimžodžių rinkinys* (Collection of unnecessary barbarisms).[27] While it is easy for detractors to dismiss the preservers as living in the past, without their determination – even single-mindedness – the language may not have been passed on to second generation Australian-born Lithuanians and may well have been totally lost to subsequent generations.

## *Singing traditions*

That the language was not totally lost can be seen in the continuing appeal of singing groups among younger Lithuanian Australians. While they may not understand the full depth and significance of the words they sing, the very act of singing has kept alive a defining characteristic of Lithuanian cultural identity. As Rytis Ambrazevičius has written: 'If you were to ask a Lithuanian about his country's traditional culture, you would most likely hear about Lithuanian songs and love of singing.'[28] The lyrics of Lithuanian folk songs cover a wide variety of subjects – work, weddings, the calendar cycle, and ceremonies attached to national feasts and war – so the act of singing keeps alive a much wider cultural attachment.

By 1959 the Lithuanian Institute of Language and Literature Science Academy in Vilnius had collected 200,000 songs, 30,000 melodies and some

45,000 fairytales. Today the archives of Lithuanian folklore contain over 400,000 collected songs, reflecting the central role Lithuanian folklorists have played in preserving this important medium of folk art for future generations.[29] Given the volume and the range of songs, it is not surprising that choirs continue to play an important role in expressing Lithuanian identity.

The first choirs in Lithuania appeared at the end of the nineteenth century. In 1899, in Kaunas, the Dainos asociacija (Song association) was established, and the first choir concert was organised. The first Lithuanian mass singing gathering, initiated by Juozas Žilevičius, was held in Kaunas in 1924. It brought together around 3,000 singers and 77 choirs. The first three Song Festivals were spaced at two to four-year intervals, with a 16-year gap in the period of political unrest in the 1930s and 1940s. The festivals were restored in 1946 and were held regularly every five years. The first World Lithuanian Song Festival was held in Kaunas and Vilnius in 1994, with Lithuanians from USA, Canada, Australia, Germany, Poland, Latvia and Russia joining 391 Lithuanian choirs.[30]

The first expatriate choral group – the famous Čiurlionis's Ensemble – was formed in Vienna immediately after the exodus from Lithuania in 1944. This group performed to the general public, made Lithuanian folksong recordings at Vienna radio studios, and gave concerts to the conscripted Lithuanians in the auxiliary units of the German armed forces and, at the end of the war, to French troops. After the war the Ensemble continued its concert tours throughout Allied-occupied Germany until the period of mass migration out of Europe at the end of the decade. Some of the singers, such as Petras and Aldona Čelna, Vladas Bosikis, and Alena and Gediminas Karazija, formed the basis of the Melbourne Lithuanian choir.[31]

Other choral groups were formed at DP camps in Western Germany and Austria, where the importance of educational and cultural activities was emphasised. For Lithuanian refugees, song provided moral strength for survival while travelling on ships to the unknown Australian continent and other parts of the world. Petras Morkūnas, who came as a refugee to Australia in 1947, organised a Lithuanian men's choir on the ship *General Stuart*

*Heintzelman*. The men's choir performed on board on 23 November 1947 to commemorate Lithuanian Army Day. After their arrival in Melbourne, the choir, together with the choirs of other nationalities, sang in response to the official speeches of welcome given by the Minister for Immigration, Arthur Calwell. The same year another Lithuanian men's choir performed aboard the *Nea Hellas* to celebrate Lithuanian Independence Day. As well as the performers of the men's choir, Lithuanian children danced and sang for the other passengers.[32]

Lithuanian migrants trying to consolidate the choirs in Australia had to contend with the huge geographical distances between relocated Lithuanians in Australia as well as their heavy work commitments. But the Lithuanians settling in Australia after World War II were determined to continue their artistic traditions and singing units were established in all capital cities – though only in Adelaide, Melbourne, Sydney and Geelong have choirs maintained their existence to the present. The fact that the first Lithuanian singing groups in Adelaide and Geelong consisted of males only was a direct consequence of the Australian immigration policy of bringing in young single European males to fill labour market needs. These male choirs played a vital role in filling in the lonely evenings faced by the young and single Lithuanian men. When Lithuanian women began arriving in the 1950s, these early male singing units provided the foundation for mixed Lithuanian choirs. Soon, all Australian Lithuanian choirs consisted of male and female singers.[33]

The editor of the Australian Lithuanian weekly *Mūsų Pastogė*, Vincas Kazokas, was the first to suggest organising Lithuanian gatherings, and the first Lithuanian Art Days were held in Sydney Town Hall in 1960. The program contained singing, dancing, an evening of literature, and an arts exhibition. At the first Song Festival held as part of Australian Lithuanian Days (ALDs) at the end of December 1960, choirs from Adelaide, Melbourne, Newcastle and Sydney made up of 64 female and 63 male singers performed. In subsequent festivals the number of choirs, songs, and choristers continued to expand. In 1966 two choirs from Canberra and Geelong joined the festival.

There was not, however, a huge increase in the number of conductors, which grew from four in 1960 to just six in 1966. At the same time, the growth in the numbers of singers, from 127 in 1960 to 209 – 113 females and 96 males – in 1968 helped to nearly double the overall number of participants.[34]

Choirs were growing throughout the 1970s, but there was an underlying tension between those who took a professional approach to singing and those who joined for socialising. As Jonas Juška, the conductor of the Geelong Lithuanian choir, noted in 1969, while some choristers approached the rehearsals in a disciplined manner, others just wanted to have a good time and chat with their friends – some missing rehearsals altogether.[35] According to the Sydney Lithuanian choir conductor Vaclovas Šimkus, professionalism was further undermined in 1972, when the organisers cut short preparation time by distributing the music to the choirs just ten – rather than 15 – months before the festival.[36] In the meantime, the number of choirs at the Song Festival declined from six in 1966 to three in 1976, and the number of participants dropped from 209 in 1968 to 170 in 1976. Individual choirs were also experiencing difficulties. Because of a shortage of conductors, choirs survived only in the bigger capital cities of Adelaide, Melbourne and Sydney. In Hobart and Canberra choirs folded when none of the members could continue their preparation for the festivals – though the Geelong Lithuanian choir was revived in 1990 and is still participating in the festivals.[37]

To arrest the decline and to bridge the generation gap, a choir of 80 children was included at the 1974 Song Festival in Adelaide. It was a moment of cultural shift. Some of older generation Lithuanians who believed in being strict with children did not like to mix children in adult activities. But during the festival many felt pride watching their own children singing in the Lithuanian language. For Adelaide Lithuanian choir conductress of 20 years, it was important to give children an opportunity to learn and perform Lithuanian choral songs, and she noted that their presence at the Adelaide Festival was welcomed.[38] But the decision was taken by other conductors not to include them in future festivals, and it was another 12 years before children were allowed to be a part of the Song Festival. In 1996, when 40 children took part in the Song Festival in Melbourne, as a result of some technical difficulties and the noise made by the performing children, once again it was decided to exclude them from future festivals. This meant that children were also excluded as potential participants in the song festivals in Lithuania. Denied the opportunity of being part of the Lithuanian singing tradition, children were distanced from close involvement in a key aspect of their parents' and grandparents' culture.

There were, however, other developments that encouraged younger Australian Lithuanians to take a greater interest in the song festivals. In 1972, after 20 years of cultural isolation, Australian Lithuanians were for the first time entertained by professional Lithuanian singers from the Chicago Lithuanian opera. Two years later the American Lithuanian composer Bronius Budriūnas was invited to conduct at the song festival in Sydney, where he shared his choral experiences with Australian Lithuanian musicians and choristers.[39] Introduced to American Lithuanian cultural achievements, Lithuanians in Australia were eager to embrace artists from their homeland, not only to enrich the programs of Australian Lithuanian Days, but also to attract greater audiences. In the 1980s, instrumental, choral and dance groups from Lithuania were hosted in Australia. The inclusion of groups and solo performers from the homeland was not without its detractors. Having lived under Soviet rule, they were viewed by some Australian Lithuanians as being partly Russianised, and there were accusations that they used too much Russian jargon and praised the easy lifestyle under Soviet rule. Some Australian Lithuanians boycotted guest performances altogether, making the artists feel unwelcome and putting on hold the high expectations of developing closer ties with Lithuanian artists.[40]

But other visitors from overseas were included in Australian Lithuanian Day programs. In 1982, the 49-strong Los Angeles Lithuanian youth group Spindulys (Sunbeam) injected Australian Lithuanian youth with a heightened interest in Lithuanian culture.[41] In the 1990s, professional groups from Lithuania played a vital role in attracting bigger ALDs audiences. Their magnificent performances introduced younger Australian Lithuanians to the traditions of their parents' homeland, now no longer refracted only through the diasporic lens and its preoccupation with preserving pure Lithuanian traditions. The fact that invited guest performers were arriving from a free Lithuania also made a difference to elderly Australian Lithuanians who warmed to the performances and the performers. The result was Australian Lithuanians were brought closer to current traditions of their homeland, and by buying and listening to records and CDs of the visiting groups, or by communicating directly with the performers, their knowledge of cultural changes in the homeland was broadened.

As we have seen in this chapter, Lithuanian language usage and singing traditions, detached from the homeland, took on different meanings. This mirrors the different constructions of *lietuvybė* in Lithuania and Australia among different generations and groups of Lithuanians discussed in previous chapters. It confirms that Lithuanian identity and its maintenance is not only moveable and malleable, but also contingent on the particular personal construction of individuals. As we have seen, not only the Lithuanian language, but also national and cultural activities have been and continue to be constructed in hybridised and creolised ways – whether in the homeland or in Australia. To borrow from Benedict Anderson, the Lithuanian community in Australia is an imagined community, with *lietuvybė* meaning different things to different members of the community. That includes my own understanding of *lietuvybė*, and in the following, final, chapter, I offer a personal account of what it has meant for me as I have made the transition as a recent arrival from Lithuania to Australia.

CHAPTER 6

# Where do I stand?

Previous chapters were based on the responses of other Lithuanian migrants I interviewed in the course of earlier research. I have tried to be accurate in my accounts of what they told me in questionnaires and interviews. I cannot deny that as researcher and writer I have mediated their 'voice', and that how I have represented it is inevitably refracted through my own understanding, values and aspirations, disappointments and fears. I have attempted to be fair and honest in how I have dealt with the information they shared, but no writer can fully step outside of herself in what she writes. In this final chapter I want to reflect upon where I stand in relation to *lietuvybė* by sharing extracts from a partially autobiographical novel I wrote for my PhD about what it means for an individual to uproot oneself from Lithuania to Australia.

My personal identity as a Soviet Lithuanian citizen helped me create the protagonist of my novel, who is also a product of the Soviet era. The parallels and similarities between me and Daina, as well as the dates, places, events, and patterns of behaviour of Daina and all the novel's other characters, are the creation of my imagination. But while fictional, the story is nonetheless true at a deeper psychic level, where it is fair to say that Daina's identity reflects my own, both as a product of Soviet society and in terms of my experience of life in Australia.

In 'Torn: the story of a Lithuanian migrant' as much as in my previous 'factual' research, my aim has been to explore the influence of migration on people's identities. I chose fiction as the vehicle for telling the stories of Australia's Lithuanian diaspora because it allowed me to provide an insight into the lives of Lithuanian migrants in a form with which all readers are familiar. We all use narrative in our everyday lives to make sense of what is going on around us, and what our role is in the greater scheme of things. The novel provided a vehicle for me to reflect on and compare postwar Lithuanian refugee experiences with my own experiences as a more recent Lithuanian migrant to Australia.

I am not claiming to be the mouthpiece of other recent arrivals. We all have our own particular stories to tell, which, while sharing features in common, are ultimately unique. As perhaps the first attempt by a recent Lithuanian migrant to create an imaginary piece of writing on what it meant to arrive in Australia, my hope is that it will encourage others to put pen to paper (or, more likely, finger to keyboard) to share their experiences in either a 'factual' or 'fictional' mode.

The novel is a creative exploration of the Lithuanian migrant experience in the diaspora between the 1980s and 1990s, when the political, socio-economic and cultural environment radically shifted under Mikhail Gorbachev's *perestroika.* Gorbachev's political agenda allowed member countries of the USSR to loosen their ties with Russia, which resulted in Lithuania proclaiming its independence in 1990.

The story revolves around two main characters – a postwar generation Lithuanian Algis and his great-niece Daina, who joins him in Australia in 1986. Algis, as a postwar Lithuanian refugee, was among the Displaced Persons who came to Australia after World War II. Daina represents the new Lithuanian arrivals from Soviet Lithuania who started to settle here from the 1970s onwards. Due to differences in age, education and life values, Algis and Daina often misunderstand each other, and through their interaction we can discern the complex layers of nostalgia and different attitudes towards their homeland and the Lithuanian community in Australia.

The novel speaks to the reader through Daina's voice. Initially she views the world through the prism of a Soviet citizen, but, influenced by the different experiences of life in Australia, Daina begins to rediscover herself. Or perhaps I should say she begins to discover a new self – yearning on the one hand for her homeland and the familiar, and on the other trying to readjust to her new life away from home.

A well-educated woman, Daina finds herself looking after Algis as well as working on his property, trying to reconcile her experience of life in her new country with what she had expected it would be. Each time she hears singing in Lithuanian at parties or concerts at Lithuanian House she vicariously returns 'home' and suffers anew the pain of loss. She misses her previous lifestyle, her family and friends. Even the national celebrations she previously had ignored assume an enhanced significance. In desperation Daina turns to music and poetry, through which she transports herself back to her homeland and she experiences – or perhaps constructs – a sense of her former self.

Daina is acutely aware of how postwar Lithuanians do not like to be around Soviet citizens like herself. She has to reconcile their claim to have fled Stalin's regime and deportations with the Soviet-inspired perception back home that those who fled were 'Nazis', 'fascists' and 'undesirable elements'. She is confused. Confused by her great-uncle's protestation that all they did was run away from the war for a short time until the Russians had left Lithuania and the American liberators had arrived. Confused by the discomfort of the postwar nationals regularly labelled negatively by people who remained in Lithuania. Confused by her own treatment at the hands of Australian Lithuanians.

For the first four years in Australia Daina lives with her great-uncle, whom we are introduced to in the following extract. However, after she gets pregnant and does not reveal to her great-uncle who the father is, the attitude of Algis – a man with strict patriarchal upbringing who cannot countenance sex before marriage – changes. After suffering a miscarriage, Daina is rushed to hospital. She does not return to Algis and stays instead with her friend Dorothy. Dorothy helps Daina obtain a housecleaner's job. Coincidently, the house she comes to clean belongs to a Lithuanian named Gintas. Living in his house and looking after him she finds happiness.

Two years later, when Gintas passes away, she visits her great-uncle. Everything has changed. His animals are gone. His farmhouse is deserted. She is not welcome. Daina decides to return to Lithuania, which she has not seen for six years. And, with what she finds there, she is greatly disillusioned.

## Excerpts from 'Torn: the story of a Lithuanian migrant'

*

### *May 1986*

After lunch Daina opened her suitcase and presented her great-uncle Algis with various gifts she had brought from home – a loaf of bread, a bottle of vodka, a linen tablecloth, a book of Lithuanian photographs and an amber rosary.

'How did you manage to get this through customs?' Algis said as he brought the loaf close to his nostrils.

'I don't know. I just walked through the 'Nothing to Declare' exit and that was it. Nobody asked me anything. Should I have told them about the bread?'

'Never mind, never mind,' he replied, patting the loaf. Tears were rolling down his cheeks. Then he put the rosary around his neck.

'Your gifts have taken me back in time,' he said. 'When the war broke out we didn't know who would win – the Germans or the Russians. The year before it ended, there was a lot of confusion. We feared for our lives. Our family home was bombed.'

'I would have died of fear,' Daina said.

'Everybody was frightened. There was so much uneasiness and it led to people running away to try and find safety. We found ourselves on a road to Germany. There were no borders, the observation decks deserted, thousands of people crowding the DP camps. We lived in three different DP camps.'

'What does DP stand for?' Daina asked.

'Displaced Persons,' he replied.

'Ah.'

'Anyway, when the Germans lost the war and the camps began to close down, we were forced to emigrate – returning to Lithuania was out of question. We would've been shot by the Russians who, by that time, were spreading propaganda about Lithuanians living abroad. They said that we were the traitors.'

'How can you be traitors if you ran for your life?'

'It's all about politics, Daina. We are traitors and you are communists, so to speak. The Russians completely control our homeland, and brainwash Soviet citizens like you.'

'I didn't know Lithuania was under Russian control,' Daina said.

'Most are afraid to talk, that's why you don't know things. People back home are a bright and happy lot, helping the Soviets to build a classless society. I'm very relieved I escaped. I chose Australia as my temporary home but ended up living here for more than forty years.'

'I see.'

As Daina listened to Algis, she regretted that her grandparents and parents hadn't told her these stories.

'But you could come back to Kretinga and stay with us, surely?'

'You can hardly fit into the tiny government flat yourselves. It's too late anyway. I built this house with my own hands – not one, but two stories. I have the animals, the car, all my friends are here, and besides, how can I leave my wife's grave? It's been ten years now,' he said.

'That means I was fourteen when she died. I remember my parents mentioning this to me. You must be so lonely.'

'Yes. Well. I had to adjust to a bachelor's life.' He lifted his cup from the table and suggested they sit in the lounge room to watch television.

'We'll talk more about this and many other things later,' he said.

Overwhelmed by the smell of fresh air, the openness of the land, and Algis' hospitality, Daina had forgotten that she'd hardly slept during her journey. But by late afternoon, she couldn't keep her eyes open and fell asleep on the couch.

The following night, Algis' house was full of visitors. To celebrate Daina's arrival, he'd invited some of his Lithuanian friends for dinner. Rimvydas and his wife, Ona, were an elderly couple about Algis' age. Ona, like Daina's grandmother, had grey hair gathered into a bun. She was slender and her face was pale. She wore a white silk blouse, dark cardigan and black slacks. Daina remembered that her grandmother never approved of women wearing pants. 'A lady should always be a lady – not a man,' she used to say. Rimvydas was tall. He wore a dark suit and a light-blue shirt with a tie. He also wore a vest underneath his unbuttoned jacket. His hair was wavy and white.

The second couple, Jonas and Zosė, wore identical green jumpers and slacks. Zosė's short hair was tightly curled. They both had chestnut hair. They must be applying the colour at the same time, sharing the dye, helping each other to dye their hair, Daina thought. Zosė gave her a bunch of white lilies. She said they were from their garden.

Daina was taken aback when she saw that the guests had also brought food – herrings, an apple cake and alcohol. In Lithuania the hosts provided all the food and drinks. She commented on this to Algis' friends.

'But it's good to bring what we love to eat. Algis usually feeds us bacon and eggs. He's a single man and not a very good cook,' Zosė replied, making everybody giggle.

Algis invited them to sit down and filled their glasses. Soon his guests began to sing the old Lithuanian songs, 'Stok ant akmenėlio' and 'Ar aš tau sese nesakiau?'.

After a few drinks the men wiped their tears away and raised their voices louder and louder. Daina didn't understand why they were so upset.

'Rimvydas and Jonas came to Australia alone, without their families,' Algis explained to her. 'To this day they feel guilty about leaving their partners behind. But their loved ones either died or disappeared during the war. Their lives would've been different if not for that stupid war. We, Lithuanians, have always been reluctant to move around or change our addresses. It's in our blood and in the blood of our ancestors to stay put, to plough our land, to harvest it, to grow the vegetables and fruit, and to care for our animals. We love agriculture; we are attached to our land.'

'I know,' Daina said. 'I was born and raised in a village-like Kretinga. But I think it's boring to stay put. That's why I wanted to study in a capital city and get away from the vegetable gardens and the same view. It's so provincial. I've always wanted to see the world.'

'You're young and naïve and don't know what you are saying,' Algis replied.

'What do you mean?'

'Well, life on my farm is very provincial, and there is nothing much here to see.'

'Aren't you planning to show me Australia?'

'Yes, I will, a little bit at a time,' he said, smiling.

His friends asked Daina about Lithuania. They had many questions about the homeland and people they remembered from their towns and villages back home, but she didn't recognise any of the names.

'How is life in Lithuania?' Rimvydas asked, putting his empty glass on a table.

'Good. My parents and my grandmother are healthy. We have good neighbours.'

'Our neighbours were the opposite,' Ona said. 'They turned out to be spies and reported us to the Russians. We were lucky to escape before they captured us.'

'But why would they take you away?' Daina asked.

'For no reason at all.' Ona said. 'I suppose for being good farmers.'

Daina continued after a pause. 'My mother and grandmother knit gloves, hats, scarves and socks which sell well at the market. My father works in a factory. And I work as a theatre producer. So, we are content.'

'That doesn't sound like what we've been told about our homeland. Some of our friends who returned to Lithuania in the late seventies and early eighties were greatly disappointed,' Jonas said, exhaling a long and narrow stream of smoke. 'They felt they were constantly being watched. They were not allowed to travel outside the capital and even discovered tiny microphones attached to the night lamps in their hotel rooms.'

'I've walked past Vilnius' International Hotel many times, not realising what was going on inside,' Daina said.

'I will tell you something,' Rimvydas said. 'My friend Kazys stayed at the hotel in Vilnius when he visited. Every night, he addressed the lamp in his bedroom saying: 'Good night, my lovely lamp. Let's have a rest. No news for you today,' before switching it off. He wanted to let them know he knew they were listening. The lucky ones snuck out to the countryside to see their properties, but found that their homes were in poor shape. Strangers, apparently Russians, had moved onto their land; they were working and ploughing their land.'

'Or drinking their life away and not worrying about the weeds,' Ona added. 'My sister wrote to me that our house in Smilgiai is collapsing, and that four different families, including our ex-servants, are living there in the space made for one family. How can we claim it back? I feel sorry for them too, because they have nowhere else to go, and even worse, because the houses belong to the government – nobody cares if they deteriorate.'

'That's terrible,' Daina said.

'That's right. Do you think we are happy that our relatives were forced into collective farming and their land taken away? We know that people steal the government's property and produce from the collective farms, so-called *kolkhozes*, then sell them privately, just to get by,' Zosė said.

'How come the Soviets let you out?' Jonas asked, and Daina admitted to them that her friend's father, a prominent diplomat, had helped her to obtain the visa.

'Is he a communist?' Ona wanted to know.

'I'm not sure,' Daina replied.

'He must be. There is no other way if you want to have a good job, a flat, a car or to go abroad. We know. We learn everything through the *Amerikos balsas* radio program,' Rimvydas said, raising his dark eyebrows. He had a sad expression on his wrinkled face.

'I am blessed to be one of the luckiest people. I can't even believe I am in Australia!' Daina exclaimed. 'I hardly knew anything about it before I arrived. There was no information about it in the local library. Also, Algis didn't mention much about Australia or Australians in his letters. How happy I am that his invitation has served as a ticket to an adventure.'

'How did you organise her coming?' Ona asked Algis.

'I invited my sister as well, but Roma can't travel. Although she is four years younger than me, she has more serious health issues. So, she suggested Daina should come by herself, and I am glad she is here. She is young and fit and can help me around the farm.' Algis was beginning to slur his words. While the women had been sipping champagne, the men had managed to finish six bottles of beer, a bottle of vodka and half a bottle of cognac. Daina wasn't surprised. In Lithuania drinking was a huge problem. The party continued late into the night, ending with hugs and kisses outside. Back home only close relatives kissed and Daina felt uncomfortable, especially when Rimvydas kissed her on the lips. He smelt of vodka, onion and perspiration. His tie was undone and his clothes stained. She spat on the grass, wiping her mouth with the back of her hand.

When they were all gone, Daina helped Algis clear away the dirty dishes, cigarette butts and empty bottles. He went to bed but she wasn't sleepy. She was amazed that Algis' friends, especially the men, after so many years remained guilty and sad. The women had been friendly and chatty but nosey.

She stood at the kitchen window, trembling with excitement at the possibility of a new life. She gazed down the long driveway, framed by gum trees, wondering what Australia had in store for her. She grabbed Algis' coat, turned the lights off, opened the front door and walked towards the trees, fascinated and frightened by their height. She wished she could climb one of them and sit on the highest branch. But she knew it would be in vain because it was so dark she wouldn't be able to see anything.

'I have plenty of time for that,' she said, hugging the closest gum tree, feeling the silky surface of its trunk. Taking in its gentle acid, Daina sat under the tree. Before long she drifted off to sleep.

*

## *October 1986*

Finally Algis announced they were going to the Lithuanian Club in North Melbourne for Sunday lunch. Daina was excited. She put on her linen dress, amber necklace and beige shoes.

'Most people get to the Club after mass,' Algis explained as they drove towards the city. 'After lunch they sit at tables or at the bar for hours. That's how we keep in touch.'

'I like that.'

'Of course, we also gather for funerals. It's our tradition here to drape the national flag of yellow, green, and red over the coffin and sing the anthem – both forbidden in Soviet Lithuania – when the body is lowered into the grave.' He paused for a minute. 'Each time someone dies, we all think: one more of us gone. Who will be the next to go? Why do we have to die here? It is a horrible thought of being laid to rest in such heavy clay soil, so far away from home. Oh, God, give us mercy.'

'Why haven't you taken me to the Club earlier?' Daina asked, trying to distract Algis from his sombre mood. 'I am looking forward to meeting people closer to my age.'

'I don't want you to fall in love with a young man and forget about me,' he replied jokingly. Algis parked his car in Errol Street, in front of the Lithuanian Club sign. When they entered through the heavy wooden door, Daina noticed the walls were covered in photographs of Lithuania – of towns, churches, and dark green forests of the countryside. There were also photos of singers, dancers and children dressed in national costumes.

'These are the local Lithuanians,' Algis explained.

'This is you,' Daina turned toward him pointing at the group photo, but he'd already moved on and she hurried to join him.

It was Sunday lunchtime and the bar was crowded. People were sitting at tables and at the bar talking and sharing jokes. They drank beer, wine and vodka. Some stood around and watched the billiard players. There was a pleasant aroma of bacon and butter. A long lane of people ordering their meals stretched from the kitchen across the dining room blocking the main entrance. Daina noticed that her favourite dishes *cepelinai* and *bulviniai blynai* were on the menu.

She was happy to be surrounded by the sound of her native language, and yet, on careful listening she noticed new words and phrases. Standing at the bar, she overheard two women discussing Queensland accommodation prices. They used a combination of English and Lithuanian words. But there was more to it – they often added the Lithuanian endings to the English words or reshaped Lithuanian words to sound more English. Thus, hotel became *hotelis*. But hotel in Lithuanian was *viešbutis*. Listening to them speak made Daina laugh and she had to move away.

Daina purchased a portion of *cepelinai* at the counter and collected them from the kitchen. On the way back she accidentally bumped into a young woman. They apologised to each other and introduced themselves. To Daina's surprise her new acquaintance had also only recently-arrived from Lithuania. Her name was Saulė. She was an accountant from Kaunas, and in Australia visiting her aunt.

'I work close to the Laisvės alėja,' Saulė said.

'I worked at the Cultural Centre as a theatre producer in Kaunas before coming here,' Daina said.

They were about to take up seats at the empty table when Algis, who had been drinking at the bar, noticed them.

'Don't sit here girls. This is Kovas' table. Sit over there, that's my table,' he pointed towards the middle of the hall.

'Do you have to pre-book the seats?' Saulė asked.

'No, but some people sort of claim their 'own' tables. We respect that. Everybody keeps to their group, eight to ten friends sitting together,' Algis explained.

Saulė and Daina glanced at each other and shrugged their shoulders, following him to another table. Daina noticed that a number of people were staring at them.

'Who are these young women?' an elderly man with thick glasses asked Algis.

'This is my niece Daina and this young lady is ... ?'

'My name is Saulė, from Kaunas. I am visiting my aunt in Melbourne.'

'What's her name?' a couple of people asked.

'Milda Žeimienė.'

'Ah, we know Žeimienė,' others replied.

'My dear friends, they both arrived recently from Lithuania: Saulė from Kaunas and my great-niece from Kretinga. You may want to know what's going on there, so come closer,' Algis said. A crowd began to form around the table and Daina felt too shy to eat.

Most of them were in their sixties and seventies. The older women were dressed as if they just arrived from a Lithuanian village. Their lips were pale, their hair was straight or in tiny curls, and they wore plain clothes. Some wore hats or berets. Some wore scarves around their neck. There were a few middle-aged women – pretty women with their make-up, blond hair and fair skin. These women looked as they had never been out in the sun. They all wore jewellery: the younger ones gold, the older women amber beads. One woman wore such a huge necklace that it pulled her neck forward. The younger men were dressed in shirts, pants and jumpers, but the elderly men wore suits. Most of them were blue-eyed and blond; some of the older men were bald or had little grey hair. Daina could see that some men coloured their hair in brown or black. They look strange, she thought, regretting not being able to share this discovery with Saulė. Everybody was still looking at them.

'Do you always wear much amber jewellery?' Saulė asked a woman, who introduced herself as Agota. Daina turned towards them and listened in.

'Usually we don't,' Agota replied. 'But during our national celebrations, we put on one or two rows of amber beads, and a brooch or a pendant. Our men wear their woven ties with the national designs.'

'That's so impressive to see you following traditions,' Saulė said.

'How hard was it to get out?' a bald man standing next to Algis asked.

'Not hard, especially because all my family lives in Lithuania,' Daina replied.

'Mine too, the same,' Saulė said.

'The Soviet authorities are reluctant to let people who don't have any relatives in Lithuania go abroad. Russian officials are especially hard on people whose family members have been deported to Siberia,' Algis added with authority, others around them nodding their heads.

'Are you planning to go back, girls?' a woman asked. Daina noticed she was wearing a linen blouse and a see-through amber necklace.

'Yes, I am,' Daina replied.

'Me too,' Saulė nodded.

People sitting around the table began enquiring about their friends and relatives.

'Do you know my brother Petraitis from Kretingalė?'

'What about the Poškaitis' family from Skuodas?

'Do you know Bitinas from Klaipėda?'

'Saulė, you live in Kaunas – I worked there, maybe you know my colleagues – Dovydėnas, Morkūnas, Sasnauskaitė?'

'Do you know any of the Gružys' family from Telšiai?'

'Norvydienė from Kretinga?'

Saulė and Daina stared at them and then at each other with surprise.

'I am sorry. I never heard of these people and some of these names are more common, I don't know if they are the people you are looking for,' Saulė said.

'There were no such names in my neighbourhood,' Daina replied, realising that people surrounding them were disappointed. They wanted to hear about the persons they had known before they had left Lithuania.

Saulė and Daina were able to sneak outside. As they stood in the hallway they shared their disbelief at the old-fashioned attitudes of those they spoke to. They agreed that entering the Melbourne Lithuanian Club was like stepping far back in time.

'It's as if time stopped in the 1940s. As if they have created a second Lithuania here, with their own thinking and hybridised language,' Daina said.

'They are definitely removed from the current times and have little idea of what's going on around them,' Saulė said.

'They have even less idea what is going on in Lithuania,' Daina added.

'How can they ask us about people in their towns? How can we know?' Saulė wondered. 'I suppose their desire to have any news from home is so strong.'

'What about their faces?' Daina asked.

'What about them?'

'It seems that elderly people look much younger here than back home. And their teeth are white and straight,' Daina said.

'That's because their life is much better in Australia, don't you think?'

'Agree.'

They both felt closely watched. They had to be careful how they phrased their sentences and who they socialised with.

'It's like living with our grandparents or parents. I feel like I am being constantly scrutinised,' Saulė said.

'Me too. Algis' friends acted strangely in my presence as if they didn't trust me.'

'Have you noticed there are hardly any young faces around?' Saulė said.

'No, but can you blame them?'

Algis' friends were still there, at the same table. They resumed the conversation about the past.

'After the war, the Soviets forced people into *kolkhozes* and demanded they grow corn. Lithuanians had never grown corn and all the pesticides they were made to spray destroyed the quality of our soil,' said a fair-haired man with a longish face. He was holding his glass tightly between his fingers, and gulped down his vodka once he had finished speaking.

'It's true. Everything belongs to the Soviet Lithuanian government,' Saulė said.

'It used to be private land, passed from generation to generation. The Russians took what was ours,' said a short man with a tipsy voice. 'We have no right to our own properties.'

A couple of women, Stasė and Rima, came forward to greet the young guests. They complimented Daina and Saulė on their looks.

'You have a thick long plait, Saulė, and such expressive eyes. They remind me the colour of the Baltic sea,' Rima said.

'Oh, thank you,' Saulė blushed. 'I am not used to compliments. In Lithuania people try to blend in; nobody says things like that. It makes me feel embarrassed.'

'Ah, don't be so shy,' said Rima.

Stasė turned to Daina.

'I've never seen a woman with such a healthy looking, glowing face. When I was young I used to spread honey on my face or bathe it in milk. That's how well off my family was. I could afford it!'

'I see, I don't do any of that. It must be the Whittlesea weather that does wonders for my skin,' Daina replied with a joyful smile. 'And I also love the Australian honey.'

'That's why your eyes are the colour of honey,' said a softly-spoken man, winking at Daina.

She giggled, putting her hand over her mouth. She was taken aback hearing these compliments, as she knew that Saulė, whose name meant sun, was the beautiful one – warm and sunny, like her name.

'You are both good-looking, just like we were once …' Stasė began, but she started to sob and couldn't continue.

'She lost her daughter during the war,' Algis whispered to Daina. Daina felt uncomfortable, as if she had done something wrong.

'These girls make a fabulous picture among you, *seni gandrai*,' the barman said, addressing the men as he wiped the table and collected the empty glasses. 'Behave, you drunkards, and treat these two young ladies with respect!' He shook his dirty cloth in the air. A bottle of vodka appeared on the table and people lifted their glasses, drinking to better times and the hope of one day returning to a free Lithuania ... A group of them broke into song about their homeland where their dreams were brighter and their future was full of promises; where their loved ones lived. They talked of their yearning for the sap of the birch tree, to see the seagulls flying above the Baltic Sea and the beauty of amber. When the glasses were empty, people embraced each other and sat around in a tight circle, swaying to and fro, moving their feet to the sound of their own voices. They knew the words of their beloved folk songs: about a young maiden and a brave man galloping towards her on a white horse; about war and death; about the beauty of their old country. Daina and Saulė joined in the singing.

A tall man wearing a checked tie asked Daina, 'Why don't you want to stay in Australia for good?'

'I feel foreign here,' Daina admitted. 'You've just told me that you experience the same feelings yourselves. It makes me wonder – if you are unable to adjust after all these years, it may be impossible. Your stories are about unfulfilled dreams. I have never felt so sad. Reading my great-uncle's books and listening to his friends' stories has made me nostalgic for things I thought I never cared about.'

'True,' Rima said. 'Here we treasure everything Lithuanian, because once we go outside the Club walls, it's another world.'

'You're right.'

'She is, isn't she?'

'Definitely,' everybody agreed.

Before Daina left the Club she visited the library and was surprised to find so many Lithuanian books. She selected a few and was told not to rush to return them.

*

## *1987*

One sunny winter morning, Algis' neighbour Mėta came for a visit. Daina stopped cleaning the bathroom and could easily overhear their conversation.

'Isn't she lovely, your great-niece?' Mėta said.

'Oh yes, she is.'

'I didn't think someone from Soviet Lithuania would be so sweet. They are well disciplined over there – like soldiers, aren't they?'

'I can't say. I haven't been back, Mėta.'

‘Me either. Whatever she does or says, she is all smiles, doesn’t shun or show disrespect to us oldies. She’s not a communist, is she?’

‘Daina is a very charming girl and of course she doesn’t belong to the Communist Party, if that’s what you’re implying. They were only forced to be the ‘grandchildren’ of Lenin, then to become pioneers and to join the komsomols in their youth. You know yourself how people back home had little choice but to comply or go to jail.’

‘Yes, I know. Oh … I’m not sure what to say. She may be a bit red, but as long as she’s not a communist, I suppose she is alright …’

‘Of course she is apolitical. She didn’t come here to collect information on us or anything like that. I checked her room and her notebook. The only thing she does is listen to the Russian news and that’s hardly a crime, is it?’

‘I agree,’ Mėta said. ‘You see, because she is Lithuanian, I want her to meet my son. He likes her already. I showed him a photo.’

‘Alright then, bring him over some time.’ Daina noticed Algis using the table to steady himself. ‘I’m feeling a little dizzy. Could you please help me into bed?’

Mėta led him to his bedroom and at that moment Daina appeared, helping him to get comfortable, tucking him in.

‘I thought you were outside,’ Mėta said.

‘I was,’ Daina lied, making her way out of the room. ‘Don’t worry about my uncle. It will pass. Lately he hasn’t been feeling well. He gets tired quickly,’ she said watching the elderly woman’s surprised face.

When Mėta left, Algis commented that he didn’t particularly like her because she was nosey. Daina hid her notebook in a new spot under her clothes in the wardrobe. She knew now that Algis had been checking her room and she didn’t want him to continue reading her private thoughts.

‘He must be so bored with his life and enjoys learning my secrets. Then he watches me and thinks, aha, I know what she is up to. I know what she thinks of me. But it’s so inappropriate. Ugly old man,’ she kept repeating aloud in her room, feeling frustrated and angry.

A week later, Mėta returned unannounced. Daina had been resting on the veranda in a folding chair, her face covered in an apricot mask.

'What happened? Are you alright? Your face is all yellow!' Mėta grabbed her by the wrist. Daina opened her eyes. She suspected that by the next day, the Melbourne Lithuanians would be gossiping about the mysterious disease she'd caught.

'I'm not ill, just having an invigorating mask to refresh my skin. The climate here is too dry and my skin is flaky.'

'I see, I see. Are you saying that you might bathe yourself in milk next?'

'I didn't say that, but of course it would be nice,' Daina teased.

'You are young and don't need any extras to look good.' Talking non-stop, Mėta tried to help Daina remove the traces of mask from her face.

'I can manage it myself,' Daina said, pushing her hand away.

Mėta placed an old suitcase near Daina's foot. When Mėta lifted the lid of the wooden case – probably a Second World War relic, Daina thought – she saw a couple of moths fly out. The strong smell of perspiration and dampness made her sneeze; she found it nauseating.

'I brought you something. Look at this coat, a cardigan, just look at this green evening dress with loose sleeves and a high neck. Feel the softness of this material!' Mėta exclaimed, planting a garment into Daina's lap. Daina sneezed again.

'You see. All these poisonous masks, they are making you unwell. You shouldn't be putting anything on your face as it may become discoloured.'

The telephone interrupted them and Daina excused herself.

'Hello.' She smiled hearing Paulius' voice. It had been two weeks since she'd responded to his ad in the Lithuanian paper, and his silence was beginning to worry her. He'd rung to ask her whether he could come for a visit and she was delighted.

'We could meet later today, about six,' she said.

'Where do you live, exactly?'

'When you arrive in Whittlesea, turn left at the roundabout, then keep driving till you reach a brown wooden gate on your right with number twenty-two written on it with chalk.'

'Lovely. See you soon then. Will you be wearing something Lithuanian?' Paulius asked.

'Maybe I'll carry a flag,' she giggled.

Mėta had been standing right behind Daina.

'Who was that?' she asked.

'It's my new friend. He's coming to visit me tonight.'

'I was hoping you'd be interested in getting acquainted with my son Ramūnas. He'd love to take you out. He is so impressed with what I've told him about your politeness and gentleness. Also, about you travelling on your own from the other side of the world where you were starving under the communists and only lived on the ideals of a perfect society. He thinks you must be very brave to manage to escape through the Iron Curtain.'

'But I didn't escape. The Moscow authorities actually let me come to visit Algis. Your ideas about me are groundless. As for the perfect society, yes, we had this dream that all, big and small, wealthy and poor, good and bad, eventually would become equal. Where we wouldn't be required to pay for goods and services, where we'd eat at communal kitchens and the government would take care of us. Equal and happy – a classless society is the goal of communism; it's a goal that we haven't quite reached yet. We've only progressed into the second stage of socialism, meaning that no matter what job one does in an organisation, most of us receive the same wages. That's the way we are aiming to achieve fairness and equality.'

'Do you really believe what you say?' Mėta asked in a fearful voice, squinting at Daina with her muddy eyes.

'Maybe or maybe not, but the citizens of Lithuania, like citizens of the other republics that belong to USSR, don't question this set of values.'

'I'm never going back to Lithuania,' Mėta said.

'Where did you originally come from?' Daina asked.

'I was born and raised in the village of Girkaliai near the famous seaside resort of Palanga. My sister is still there. We had a wonderful childhood – our parents used to take us to the beach, where we enjoyed swimming and building sandcastles. Being five years older than my sister, I'd create my castle and then help Rožė finish hers. Our parents would come to inspect our artwork, rewarding us with ice cream. Oh, how I miss those carefree days.'

'Where are your parents now?'

'They were taken away. I never heard from them.'

'That's so sad.'

'Luckily the night they were deported, I was away in Vilnius and my sister was staying with our aunt in Šiauliai. We survived, but were separated. I love my little Rožytė. She is seventy-five now. She only survives because of the parcels I send her.'

'What do you send?'

'Second-hand shoes and clothing.'

'Like what you brought today?'

'Yes, similar.'

'But people over there can buy ordinary clothes. Food is a problem,' Daina said.

'Well, Rožė has never mentioned not wanting clothes …'

'How could she? It would upset you, wouldn't it?'

'Are you saying that I should send her other items? I know that some of my friends send sugar and rice.'

'Not sugar or anything heavy like rice, but dried fruit and vitamins and other essentials like toilet paper and medication. I am sure your sister would be happier with those sorts of things.' She felt like adding – rather than wearing stinky, moth-eaten items – but she didn't for Algis' sake. 'Don't think badly of Lithuania,' she said instead. 'Personally, my life was alright there. My education was free. I could easily eat my three-course dinner for a ruble while earning 130 rubles a month. My rent used to be 15 rubles per month. Bread only cost 30 kopeks a loaf. I was able to have two part-time jobs on top of my main position. It was hard to juggle, but possible. The reward was great – every summer my friends and I could afford to travel around the Soviet Union.'

'But we've heard that pensioners can't survive. That's why I'm helping my sister,' Mėta replied. Daina observed her opening her black leather handbag. Mėta's grey hair, gathered neatly in a bun, was falling loose.

'By the way, I have something for you from Ramūnas,' she said, going through the contents of her bag. Her short thin fingers shook as she mumbled swear words *'velnias tave rautų, velnias tave rautų!'* under her breath. Finally, she took out a small blue box and offered it to Daina. Daina didn't move.

'You mustn't refuse. Have a look at it.'

'I don't even know your son. How can I take his gift?'

'Oh, that's no problem. I can show you his photo,' Mėta replied, reopening her handbag. It contained used tissues, a few lipsticks and a half eaten apple. 'Here it is.' Mėta produced a scrunched, oily photograph of her son, wiping sweat from her forehead with her used tissues and adjusting her loosened hair with a few pins.

'This photo is unclear. I can't see his face. I must start cooking for my guest now, if you'll excuse me, please.' She observed Mėta angrily stuffing the blue box and the photo in her pocket, closing the top of the suitcase she had brought, and walking towards her car. Daina noticed how well Mėta was dressed. She wore expensive-looking slacks and a light-brown blouse, buttoned up to her neck. On the middle finger of her left hand, a huge diamond ring shone, and an opal brooch was pinned to her cardigan. She placed her suitcase in the boot of her vehicle and before driving away she swore loudly at Daina:

*'Tai matai kokia komunistė atsirado!'*

*

## 1990

Daina's friend Dorothy managed to find some casual employment for Daina through a cleaning agency in Bentleigh. Daina didn't hesitate to take the job. The following morning, she knocked on the door of a red brick house with huge windows, carrying a plastic bag with detergents, cloths and sponges. An elderly man with a tiny smile answered the door.

'My name is Daina Leitaitė from the cleaning agency.'

*'Labas rytas. Gintas Storpirštis,'* he replied in Lithuanian, telling her that he recognised her nationality by her surname and her accent. 'Come in,

Daina. Do you love singing? Would you be singing, as your name implies, while cleaning?'

'No, no. My parents gave me this name without realising the meaning. I am not a good singer.'

'Here, here. Don't be modest. All Lithuanians are good singers. Would you like some coffee?'

Daina nodded, following Gintas into an ill-lit kitchen with worn-out cupboards where he poured hot water into two cups.

'Oh, you must've been waiting for me?'

'Yes. I rarely have visitors, but this morning has turned out to be very special – a young lady from Lithuania is visiting an old man who is from the same place,' he joked, winking. Daina felt at home. She told him about coming to Australia to visit her great-uncle, and that they'd had a falling out. She explained that she was now temporarily living with her friend. He didn't ask why, and she relaxed and started cleaning. She dusted, mopped the floor, scrubbed his pots and pans, and ironed, completing her tasks by early afternoon.

'You are very thorough. I want you to come again,' Gintas said, looking around the sitting room and taking his wallet out. 'Fifty dollars; this is for four hours, ten dollars an hour. Am I right?'

Daina thanked him for the money and the generous tip and promised to return a week later.

'But my house gets really dusty and I need someone to water the garden as well as to wash the curtains. Can you come back the day after tomorrow?'

'Of course I can,' Daina replied, tightly squeezing her first wage in her palm.

Soon after she moved into Gintas' house as he needed a carer. Gintas led Daina into his study.

'Who are your favourite writers?' he asked.

'I hope you won't get upset if I tell you that I enjoy Dostoyevsky, Pushkin and Tolstoy?'

'Not at all. They belong to the classics and are there to stay.'

'My favourite Lithuanian poet is Justinas Marcinkevičius.'

'You'll find *Anna Karenina*, *The Brothers Karamazov*, *The Captain's Daughter* somewhere on the top shelf. I have a few volumes of enjoyable Australian poetry here too. Are you familiar with English and American literature?'

'Not much. We didn't have access to Western literature, although I read some translations of Dumas, Balzac, Stendhal. I wish I could read more, much more and in their original language.'

'My library is at your disposal,' Gintas said, pulling the history volumes and art books from the shelves. 'All yours – read it, have it, take it, do whatever you want.'

Daina thanked him and assured him she'd be spending all her free time here in the library.

'I never saw such literature on the shelves of the bookshops or libraries in Lithuania,' she admitted.

'It's understandable. The events of the forties, fifties, sixties and seventies were kept hush hush,' Gintas replied.

She'd been in his library while cleaning, but now she was intrigued to find a large section on deportation. She'd heard so much from Algis, his friends, and from others at the Melbourne Lithuanian Club about Lithuanians being sent to Siberia. Now she thought she would find out why people had had no choice, no control over their destiny; why the Soviet leader Stalin was so strict and even sent his own family members to the death camps; why everybody was so afraid of the Soviet regime and KGB interrogations.

'I'd love to read more about things I knew nothing about before coming here,' she said to Gintas after they left his study.

That night Daina thought about Algis and their visits to the Lithuanian Club. How the postwar Lithuanians seemed strange and distant. Now she was beginning to see she had much in common with them. Their stories of loss and disappointment resembled her own life in many ways. Some of them were non-educated farmers, some had been rich, others were young school-leavers, others were established in their professions as doctors, engineers, architects, lawyers, and musicians. When they arrived in Australia in the late '40s or early '50s, they all had to work as labourers on the railways, bridges, and roads or as domestics in hospitals and hostels. Most of them never returned to doing what they knew best – to their previous professions. She understood how they felt. She liked working for Gintas but not being able to practice in her theatre producer's profession, she too had lost her self-esteem.

Daina read non-stop. She learned about her country's determination and people's strength to survive in the camps of Gulag. Alexander Solzhenitsyn's *The Gulag Archipelago* stories were English translations and difficult to understand, but personal accounts, like Liudas Dovydėnas' *Žmonės ant vieškelio*, were breathtaking. Books like Edgars Dunsdorfs' *Baltic dilemma* gave her an overview of what had happened in all the Baltic States before, during and after the Second World War; but it was the personal accounts that made her heart miss a beat. Like *For those still at sea,* the story of the Lithuanian sailor Simas Kudirka's detection that really got to Daina – how he had jumped ship, how the American Coast Guard cutter *Vigilant* had had to return him back to the *Sovetskaya Litva,* how he was tortured and beaten, and imprisoned in various labour camps, how he was finally allowed to leave Soviet Lithuania for the USA, only because of his shared luck that his mother was born there.

Usually, at the dinner table, Daina discussed what she was reading with Gintas. She was getting into the Stalinist era. The more she read the more she could recall her grandparents' conversations. When she was little, playing with her rag doll in a corner, they had talked about the hard times. Now parts of those conversations returned to her. She recalled them talking of losing everything. She had been too small to understand what they meant. Once, her grandfather showed her a scar on his left leg. He said it was from an operation in his youth. After Algis told her the truth about her grandfather, she could easily picture him being forced to dig the German trenches with other seventy-five thousand men from Lithuania. And she realised he had been lucky not killed, lucky to just have a limp for the rest of his life. She recalled what a quiet man he was, never replying back when her grandmother told him off.

When Daina was growing up, her family was reluctant to discuss the war. They sometimes whispered, or her father swore while watching the TV. She was wondering why German soldiers in the movies looked like beggars with ripped clothing and bad or no shoes. They look stupid, not like Russian soldiers who were bright and clever, whistling a song of victory and giving sweets to street children.

One night in Gintas' library Daina read about dissidents who were forcefully removed from society for their non-conforming behaviour. Sent to prison camps or mental institutions for promoting national traditions and distributing folk songs, plays or other literature, for practising and spreading their religious beliefs and for organising anti-Soviet demonstrations. She was not familiar with the word 'dissident'. She opened a page of a ragged looking book without a front cover and saw a tiny photo of dissident Nijolė Sadūnaitė, a religious freedom fighter who had ended up as a political prisoner in a concentration camp in Moldavia, where she took an active role organising camp demonstrations. Intuitively Daina recognised strong determination in Nijolė's words 'when the stomach was empty, the head was clearer, and, as a result, the prisoners' minds were clear and inventive.' Daina felt the power of her words – and understood why the other prisoners followed. She shared in the torment.

She read of another dissident Henrikas Jaškūnas, tortured in the prison of Panevėžys, and then sentenced in 1946 to twenty-five years imprisonment in Vorkuta. Vorkuta, the 'evil camp', full of people like Henrikas who'd protested against the abuse of power by the Soviets. Holding a tissue box beside her, Daina continuously wiped away her tears, imagining how he must have suffered when his teeth had been pulled out without anaesthetic, and how he didn't have a chance to say good-bye to his wife and daughters, before dying from a heart attack in 1982.

Daina could not believe she had never heard of Nijolė's or Henrikas' stories. She wondered how many books she would have to read to discover and count the names of the brave people who paved the way for her existence. She could not believe the story of the jazz musician who was declared a schizophrenic just because he wore long hair and loved a certain type of music. That innocent farmers and intelligentsia were jailed just because Russians wanted to destroy the Lithuanian nation. As she thought about what she read, the faces of the postwar Lithuanians at the Club resurfaced. Her new knowledge confirmed to Daina why they were so different. She'd come from Soviet Lithuania, but the postwar refugees had run away from the Soviets. Algis and his friends hated their power. She understood now why they were cautious of her. The word 'Soviet' was like poison to them. To them she was a product of Soviet education and mentality that they, the postwar refugees, hated so much. Gintas was now her only Lithuanian friend. He was kind and generous. He'd never shown any hostility towards her and that was so refreshing. She recalled her grandparents' saying: 'one can't put all vegetables in one basket as they don't look and taste alike.' The same with people, each person thinks and communicates in the way that's unique, she thought.

Daina heard a loud laugh outside and glanced through the half drawn curtain. Children across the road were playing in a sandpit. Someone passed on a bicycle, and a postman dropped a letter in their letter box. Soon she saw Gintas bending his knees, trying to pull the envelope from the letter box, ripping it open on the way back. His short, skinny figure, straight grey hair and tidy appearance didn't give his age away, but Daina knew he was suffering ill health. He had asthma, and chest pains. His family doctor had recommended a pacemaker operation, but Gintas had asked for more time to think about it. Daina watched how he shuffled up the stairs, slowly opening and closing the front door.

Sitting in her room, and sipping her strong Italian coffee, she realised that life with Gintas amongst his resourceful library would not last forever. She decided to value every moment acknowledging that her life in Australia was carefree compared to lives of those she was reading about in the books on Gintas' dusty selves: books that were still not accessible to the people of the Soviet Union. She was glad to be in his study, safe from the police and the KGB interrogations. At the same time she felt sad for her nationals who had risked their lives to keep and distribute the illegal literature. Forbidden brochures, journals and books were defaming the Soviet State and the socialist ideals. She'd doubted whether she could've been as brave as these people who had fought for the freedom and the independence of her homeland. Her life compared to theirs was heaven.

What surprised Daina even more was that during the years of the Soviet occupation any attempt to flee from the Soviet Union without official permission resulted in ten or fifteen years imprisonment. How fortunate she was that Gorbachev came to power in 1985, the following year introducing his policy of economic 'acceleration', and relaxing the restrictions on people venturing abroad. Of course, as a Soviet citizen, her personal profile would have been carefully checked, but she was given permission to visit her relative in Australia. She was glad the Australian Embassy in Moscow had let her out, but she realised it was only because of a friend's father that it was possible to speed-up the paper work – and even then the process took more than six months. Without the serendipity of a father of a friend she may never have found herself sitting in a comfortable house amongst the books that exposed so many of her country's secrets. She would never have been able to experience the Australian lifestyle or enjoy the exotic fruits of this continent. She knew she should be thankful for what she had. She realised how short-sighted she'd been ever considering returning to where things were politically distorted.

*

## *1992*

'I am afraid to restart my life in Lithuania. I hope I can readjust,' Daina said to her journalist friend Jovita when they met for lunch.

'Maybe your boss in Kaunas is still holding your position open for you?'

'It's funny you say that,' Daina replied. 'My mum told me that he'd rung her a couple of times, asking when I would be back. He said he had a message for me.'

'What did she say to him?'

'She said she'd let him know if I came back.'

'Did she ask about the message?'

'No.'

'You must go and see him. He may have kept your position open and you might be able to slip into it straight away.'

After the waiter brought their coffees, Jovita spoke of Daina's stories. She admitted she hadn't been able to publish them when they first began to arrive from Australia because she had been called in to see a government apparatchik and had been given a warning.

'An elderly man sat me down in his office and showed me your first letter. He told me that there was no place in Kretinga's newspaper for such fantasies. He said that stories praising Australia might spread propaganda amongst the readers and may give them the impression that life in Soviet Union was not good enough.'

Daina sat speechless, covering her mouth with her hand.

'Don't worry Daina, I was not in trouble. When I received each of your letters, sometimes opened, sometimes closed, I kept them locked in my drawer at home. When independence came, we published them all without hesitation.'

Daina was looking tense, but Jovita laughed.

'There was no way other than to think what we wanted but to do what *they* said. We never knew who the informers were and who filtered information at school, at work, or in the neighbourhood. But it's the past, Daina, cheer up!'

'I cannot believe what had happened,' Daina said watching a group of school children obediently crossing the road.

'You have lived on another planet for some time and forgot that we remained locked up.'

After an hour or so, Jovita had to return to work. Before she left, she begged Daina to write more about Australia. People of the freed homeland were keen to explore the world, but Australia remained like a faraway dreamland, and there would be a lot of interest in Daina's stories. Daina promised to bring some more writing soon.

Walking back home, she looked around Kretinga, wondering about what Jovita had said. All the hidden stories, she thought. Would they ever resurface? Would she ever know the whole truth behind the distortions and lies? She tuned into her surroundings. Kretinga's main street was full of run-down flats; passers-by with shopping bags and preoccupied faces hurried in all directions; people spoke Lithuanian much faster than before, making her aware how much the language had changed. A group of youngsters, waiting for a bus, were conversing in blended Lithuanian words, using English phrases, intermixed with the local *žemaičių* dialect. Daina wondered how much these young people cared about their ancestors' stories. Regardless of her new reality, she knew that she was home, ready to face any challenges.

Daina decided to visit her school friends. The next day she caught a bus to Klaipėda to spend some time with Regina and Ilona. Regina worked as an accountant at the superannuation office Sodra. She told Daina how poorly her boss managed transactions and how they could never balance their books. She sounded upset that democracy was coming too slowly.

'The main problem is that we wait and talk of changes that never come. We feel like blind kittens taken from their mother, weak and unsteady on our feet, unable to fend for ourselves. 'Mother' Russia is not there anymore to lean on – we are all by ourselves, but the attitude hasn't changed. You'll realise this after staying here longer.'

'I work for a modelling company,' said Ilona. 'I'm about to fly to Dubai.'

'What do you do?' Daina asked.

'Design lingerie.'

The trio had eaten their way through potatoes, carrots and chicken. Then they had a piece of *šakotis* each. Daina recalled how miserable she was the last time she tried the cake at Saulė's wedding. Today was another matter. She didn't have to miss her homeland. She was here, sipping champagne with her friends.

Regina and Ilona wanted to know about Australia.

'It's a wonderful country, girls,' Daina said after a while. 'The countryside is picturesque, the people are kind and the food is plentiful. It's a great holiday destination – to me, *only* a holiday destination. I had to work on a farm. I didn't enjoy the hot weather. Also, I longed for company. Look at us – we grew up together and have so much in common. I missed you. I missed the sound of our language. I missed the smell of real bacon, dripping with fat. I missed the fragrance of flowers. They don't have any fragrance there. No, some do, but it's very faint. Oh, I am so pleased to be back.'

'You mean, for good?' her friends asked.

'Yes.'

'How can you be so detached from reality? Don't you see what's happening here? Now everyone is just concerned for themselves, no more collectivism with a pitchfork in one hand and a red flag in another!' Regina laughed.

'Personally,' Ilona spoke, 'I've had enough of being faceless. I am designing the undies we used to be so short of!'

'Good for you,' Daina said.

'You should see my colleagues in Dubai – constantly kissing my hand, finding me new clients. And the photographers are so kind and gentle to our models, smiling at them as if they'd found a diamond – wanting photos of their bodies from all possible angles. I've never experienced anything like that, not at school, at home or at the office where I used to work. I get a lot of attention. I can't understand why you'd wish to stay here, Daina? You must've had an awful time in Australia.'

Daina changed the subject.

'What about the regained freedom?' Interrupting each other, her friends explained how the government wanted to return the country to the glory enjoyed in the twenty-two year period between the wars, but things had gone wrong.

'How can you return from collective to individual farming when the facilities are not there, equipment destroyed, goods and produce constantly stolen? As an accountant, I can see no bright future,' Regina said.

'I can,' Ilona said, 'but only when at least two generations affected by the Soviet regime have passed away.'

The friends talked into the night. Daina laughed as they told her Russian and Lithuanian jokes about the current living standards. Despite all the changes going on in their lives, deep down they were still the schoolgirls she knew. The aroma of the food they ate, the music they listened to while chatting away, the way they incorporated the Russian words into their conversation – it was what she had missed so much. That was why the last cup of coffee they shared before her departure brought tears to her eyes.

Daina caught a bus to Kaunas. She decided to surprise her colleagues at the Cultural Centre where she'd worked before leaving, and catch up with her boss. Inside the Centre she discovered long tables covered in clothing and shoes. Apparently it had been converted into a market. Even the nearby cinema was overcrowded with white goods and electrical appliances made in Poland and the United Arab Emirates. She crossed the Laisvės alėja twice and didn't meet any familiar faces. But at the Western style shopping centre Daina bumped into her cousin. Their meeting resulted in Daina getting a job at the clothing shop where Audra worked. Audra, an actress, admitted that it was difficult to get a job in her profession but she was hopeful.

The women put their heads together about how to best utilise their talents. Audra inducted Daina into her workplace culture and how they were marketing their clothing. They had to be friendly and smile at their customers.

'When I was on my own, I didn't do nearly as well,' Audra commented after calculating the week's takings. 'If we continue in the same spirit, we'll get off the ground so fast, we won't know ourselves. The whole population of Kaunas will be wearing *our* clothing!'

Daina glanced around the shop, tidied coat hangers, and adjusted scarves. She remembered seeing coats in Melbourne being sold with a free scarf. She suggested this to Audra and they ordered some giveaways to go with the main purchase: purses, pouches, stockings, handkerchiefs and hair pins. Once these extras arrived, Daina thought of children's beanies, socks, stockings and tiny make-up kits.

Daina did her best to improve the business, dealing with suppliers, checking the quality of the goods they received, and making sure they had the full range of sizes. She was good with figures and also managed the store well. She tried to be friendly to everyone, but also assertive. She didn't hesitate to express her dissatisfaction with the drivers for late deliveries or to the manufacturers for damaged stock. She realised how many valuable lessons she'd learned in Australia: how to engage in conversation with clients as they entered the shop, how to present the clothes, how to stretch a raincoat or jumper around a client's shoulders and pull it down evenly, so that it felt and looked its best. Audra and Daina made a good team, but soon Audra re-established herself at the theatre and left. Daina regretted not being able to find any work in her profession, but she soon realised that acting and going to the theatre was not people's priority. She discovered how difficult it was to find actors for her play, even though she ran her ad in *Kauno diena* newspaper for two weeks. People were struggling on low wages and living costs were high. They didn't care much for entertainment.

The new assistant, Sandra, was the opposite of Audra, openly admitting after observing Daina on the floor that she wasn't cut out for sweet talk. Sandra didn't care how many items they sold or what reputation they obtained; instead she constantly spread her misery around. She had some personal problems, and was working as a waitress at a night club, and found it hard to fit two jobs into her life.

'I have no intention of being kind. We are paid the minimum wage and no extras, why should I care?'

Listening to her, Daina began to realise that maybe, for people like Sandra, the regaining of independence had come too quickly. Maybe there should have been a longer transitional period to get into the Western lifestyle.

Daina found that after living under the Soviets for half a century, Lithuanian people had adopted their attitudes. She remembered how as a teenager she used to wait for the sales person to complete their personal conversation over the counter before being served. And how people had not objected when shop assistants let their friends squeeze in front of them. The shoppers waited twenty minutes or more to be served. Those who dared to complain were told off. Rudeness was one of the common features of everyday life. But people knew no different. The borders had been closed. She might have been happier with the new Lithuania if she hadn't had the opportunity to live in Australia. She had seen, learned and experienced more than those who had never lived abroad and felt different because of it.

'Even though Lithuania has regained its independence, customer service staff still follow the principles of the Soviet regime. Sandra, can't you see the way you behave? You make people wait for so long, they run out of patience and leave the shop; you attend to the rich clients and show them the best items, the ones that you have hidden behind the counter; you serve your friends and acquaintances first, singling them out of the queue. Our customers will spread the word about your rudeness and we'll lose business.'

'Oh, you think because you've lived in Australia, you know better. You know nothing! You are a foreigner here and your ideas and suggestions are foolish. Look at yourself. Customers don't like you. They think you are trying to sell damaged stock or something; you get right into their faces, pushing this and that at them. Who needs your capitalist scarves? They've all got scarves here – plenty – people still know how to knit. You are a naïve and immature woman!' Sandra shouted in her rough voice. Then she disappeared to the back of the shop for her hourly cigarette.

Daina didn't reply, feeling insulted and misunderstood, making comparisons between Lithuanians and Australians in her mind. She'd thought she would never want to live in Australia again, but already, after only a few months in her homeland, she'd become disillusioned. She and Sandra were the same age; they'd both grown up under the same system of values and beliefs. But they were strangers to each other. If she'd never left, never been abroad, she might be like Sandra too.

After work Daina walked through her favourite Laisvės alėja. Passers-by looked like Algis, Gintas, Mėta. Daina saw Saulė standing near the intersection and ran towards her. But it wasn't Saulė – only a stranger glancing at her with surprise. Daina wanted to scream 'Where is my home?', but the words stuck in her throat. She reached the end of the Laisvės alėja and disappeared into the crowd …

# Epilogue

Daina's disappearance into the crowd at the end of the Laisvės alėja is not the end of the story. Chapter 6 has provided fragments of the story, which is to be continued. In the Prologue, I signalled that the extracts from my novel contained in Chapter 6 paid homage to all the stories told and yet-to-be-told by countless members of the Lithuanian community in Australia. In that respect, it is perhaps fitting that I have provided just *fragments* of my story, because most of the time (perhaps all of the time) the stories we tell are always fragmented.

As Chapters 1–5 have shown, circumstances and contexts do not stand still, and the stories we tell people have to change in line with shifting circumstances and contexts. So, we can never really tell more than a fragment of an evolving story, and I offer my fragment as a metaphor for the evolving story of *lietuvybė* down under.

# Notes

## Prologue

1 For the methodological details refer to the Appendix 3: *A note on methodology*.

## Introduction

1 I am now omitting quotation marks on ‘preserve’, ‘preservation’ etc.
2 Bhabha in Rutherford 1990: 211.
3 Walker 1986: 16.
4 Mishra 1992–93: 1.
5 Hall 1993: 361.
6 Clifford 1994: 302–17.
7 Safran 1991: 87.
8 Eckermann 1994: 2.
9 Eckermann 1994: 2–3.
10 Putniņš 1981: 26.
11 Pranauskas 1998: xiii.
12 Putniņš 1981: 2.
13 Also see further discussion on ethnic origins in Putniņš 1981: 2, 4.
14 Brah1998: 18–21.
15 Hall et al. 1992: 277.
16 Hall 1990: 222, 225.
17 Bhabha in Rutherford 1990: 211.
18 Bhabha 1993: 356.
19 Hall et al. 1993: 276–7.
20 Baskauskas 1985: 60–2.
21 Baltutis 1981: 52–3.
22 Putniņš 1981: 5.

## Chapter One

1 These include: Albertas Gerutis, Genovaitė Kazokas, Richard Krickus, Thomas Remeikis, Vytas Stanley Vardys, Nicholas Riasanovsky, Robert Gellately, Ramūnas Tarvydas, Karen Dawisha and Bruce Parrott.

2 Jakštas in Gerutis 1969: 43–4; Puzinas in Gerutis 1969: 40.

3 Rose in Taškūnas 1992: 12; Riasanovksy 1993: 133–4.

4 Riasanovsky 1993: 134–5; Daugirdaitė-Sruogienė 1990: 59, 65; Kudirka 1991: 5; Rose in Taškūnas 1992: 13.

5 Jakštas in Gerutis 1969: 59; Riasanovsky 1993: 134–5; Rose in Taškūnas 1992: 13; Urban 1992: 145–6.

6 Urban 1992: 146; Jakštas in Gerutis 1969: 81; Rose in Taškūnas 1992: 13–14.

7 Daugirdaitė-Sruogienė 1990: 156.

8 Hall 1992: 277.

9 Thurston in Paliokas 2011.

10 Daukša in Brazytė-Bindokienė 1989: 24.

11 Daukša in Daugirdaitė-Sruogienė 1990: 171; Kazokas 1992: 37–8; Anderson 2006: 149.

12 Daugirdaitė-Sruogienė 1990: 191; Kazokas 1992: 37–8.

13 Daugirdaitė-Sruogienė 1990: 203–23, 251; Gordon 1996: 222; Gierowski 1986: 1–101; *Lietuvos TSR istorija* 1986: 222.

14 Rose in Taškūnas 1992: 15.

15 Vardys 1978: 16–17.

16 Ibid.

17 Remeikis 1980: 24.

18 Hope 1994: 55; Gerutis 1969: 259–60, 65.

19 Kudirka 1991: 7; Kazokas 1992: 12.

20 Kazokas 1992: 13; Andriejauskaitė 1994, 1998.

21 Tarvydas 1997: 4; Giordano 1997: 111–12; Riasanovsky 1992: 517; Gerutis 1969: 267; Vardys 1965: 115.

22 Gerutis 1969: 277–8.

23 Ibid.: 280.

24 Ibid.: 276–7; Snyder 2004: 18.

25 Budreckis in Gerutis 1969: 316–17.

26 Gerutis 1969: 280, 283–5; Matulionis 1992: 124; Gellately 2007: 292–6.

27 Gerutis 1969: 285; Taškūnas 1992: 17.

28 Vardys 1965: 16, 67–8.

29 Gerutis 1969: 286, 298.

30 Ibid.: 286, 289; Vardys 1965: 67, 71–3; Kasekamp 2010: 134–5.

31 Mackevičius 1986: 3.

32 Ibid.

33 Ibid.: 4.

34 Raštikis 1982: 338–9.

35 Kasekamp 2010: 136; also see Vardys 1965: 72; Krickus 1997: 16.

36 Matulionis 1992: 124; Krickus 1997: 16, 19.

37 Although Lithuanian historian Daugirdaitė-Sruogienė 1990: 171 indicates the number of people who escaped from Lithuania to Germany in 1944 was 100,000, according to Matulionis 1992: 124 and Taškūnas 1992: 18, that number was 80,000. However, more recent research reveals the number to be 60,000–65,000. See Kiaupa 2005: 334; Kasekamp 2010: 139; Sužiedėlis 2011: 25; Dapkutė 2012: 16.

38 Kazokas 1992: 18; *Lietuvių enciklopedija* 1955: 148.

39 Pranauskas 2003 interview, Appendix 2.

40 Kazokas 1992: 55.

41 Pranauskas 2003 interviews, Appendix 2.

42 Straukas 1983: 18; Putrimas 2001: 5; Birškys et al. 1986: 18; Jupp 1995: 70; Kunz 1988: 43, Table 4.1; Dunsdorf 1975: 27; Taškūnas 29 Sep. 2012.

43 Taškūnas 2012; Dunsdorfs 1975, 1982; Kasekamp 2010: 133; Birn 2006: 258.

44 Shtromas 1994: 100.

45 Sniečkus in Urbonaitė 2002: 13; also see Shtromas 1994: 101.

46 In Nogee 1972: 60–2.

47 Ibid.: 62.

48 Aspaturian in Remeikis 1980: 25; Krickus 1997: 25.

49 Krickus 1997: 26.

50 Remeikis 1980: 405–6; Senn 1997: 355.

51 Krickus 1997: 28–9.

52 Remeikis 1980: 25–6; Rose et al. 1988: 71, 408.

53 Dawisha & Parrott 1995: 16; Vardys 1978: 172.

54 Kudirka & Eichel 1978; Vardys 1978: 170–1.

55 Vardys 1978: 172.

56 Ibid.: 172–3.

57 Ibid.: 173–4.

58 Ibid.: 173–7.

59 *The chronicle of the Catholic Church in Lithuania* 1972; Krickus 1997: 37.

60 Krickus 1997: 38.

61 Dawisha & Parrott 1995: 16–7; Hosking 1992: 2–4.

62 Remeikis 1980: 450.

63 Ibid.: 1, 8.

64 Ibid.: 149.

65 Rose et al. 1998: 56, 82; Thom & Regan 1988.

66 Čekuolis in Krickus 1997: 27–8.

67 Ibid.: 29.

68 Mole 2012: 68; Smith 1994: 121, 128–9; Dawisha & Parrott 1995: 17–18; Hroch 1996: 70–1.

69 Smith 1994: 305; Krickus 1997: 50, 72; Rubas 1992: 27.

70 Landsbergis in Krickus 1997: 62; Rubas in Taškūnas 1992: 28–9. *Lietuva: dokumentai, liudijimai, atgarsiai* 1991; also see Lithuanian Supreme Council of the Republic Act of the reestablishment of the State of Lithuania, viewed 1 July 2016: http://www.lrs.lt/datos/kovo11/aktas.htm.

71 Kramer 2009: 108–9; Rubas in Taškūnas 1992: 37.

72 Landsbergis in Krickus 1997: 204.

73 Krickus 1997: 195–6, 200, 202; Johannsen & Pedersen 2011: 343.

74 Astrauskas 28 April 2003: 4; See Lithuanian Bureau of Statistics: 'Population at the beginning of the year by ethnicity, statistical indicator and year', viewed 2 Jan. 2013.

## Chapter Two

1 Gellately 2007: 589.

2 Ginsburgs 1957: 354; Saidel 1984: 109–10.

3 Bethell 1974: 25.

4 Zake 2010: 31.

5 Bethell 1974: 8–15, 22–30, 35–40, 55, 64–74.

6 Plume & Plume 2004: 149.

7 Birn 2006: 258; Also see Cohen & Kapsis 1977: 637–53; Garrett 1978: 301–22.

8 Kasekamp 2010: 133.

9 L'Hommedieu 2011: 55.

10 Jupp 1995: 71; Šeštokas 2010: 64.

11 Ibid.: 70.

12 Holt 1953: 3; Also see Appleyard 1972.

13 Jupp 1995: 73.

14 Drawing from my questionnaire and interview responses as part of my MA research.

15 Pranauskas 2003 interviews, see Appendix 2.

16 Putniņš 1981: 1–2.

17 Taškūnas 1980: 5.

18 Šeštokas 2010: 130; Also, on mental anguish see Šeštokas 2010: 111–14, 143, 166–7; on migrant mistreatment see Tarvydas 1997: 21, 24, 29.

19 Šeštokas 2010: 60, 68–9, 113.

20 Pranauskas 1998 interview, see Appendix 1.

21 Pranauskas 2003 interview, see Appendix 2.

22 Ibid.

23 Tarvydas 1997: 22.

24 Pranauskas 2003 interview, see Appendix 2.

25 Birškys et al. 1986: 26.

26 Tarvydas 1997: 21, 18.

27 Kunz 1988: 49, Figure 4.3; Tarvydas 1997: 7.

28 Pranauskas 1998: 7; Šeštokas 2010: 129–30; Pranauskas 1998 interview, see Appendix 1; Tarvydas 1997: 18–23.

29 Kunz 1988: 241; Tarvydas 1997: 21.

30 Kunz 1988: 132–3, 76. Also see Kuzin 1972: 13–14.

31 Kazokas 1992: 21–2; Dunsdorfs 1975: 28.

32 Šeštokas 2010: 126.

33 Kunz 1988: 257–58.

34 Pranauskas 2003 interview, see Appendix 2.

35 Kamien 2007: n.p.

36 Ibid.; Birškys et al. 1986: 21–2.

37 Birškys et al. 1986: 21.

38 See Zubrickas 1999: 116–67, 302–3, 321–2, 615–16; 427–8; Baltutienė et al. 1990: 66, 77, 90–1, 134–5; Pranauskas 2003 interview, see Appendix 2.

39 Pranauskas 2003: 51.

40 Kazokas 1992: 58; Krupinski cited in Collins 1991: 56; Kunz cited in Collins 1988: 56.

41 Kazokas 1992: 55.

42 Pranauskas 2003 interviews, see Appendix 2.

43 Ibid.

44 Ibid.

45 Ibid.; Pranauskas 2003: 53.

46 Pranauskas 2003 interview, see Appendix 2.

47 Ibid.

48 Ibid.

49 Ibid.

50 Ibid.

51 Krupinski et al. 1973: 31, 35; Putninš 1981: 34–47.

52 Kunz 1998: 229, 236; Tarvydas 1997: 90; Birškys et al. 1986: 31.

53 Kazokas 1992: 22.

54 Straukas 1983: 20.

55 'Lietuvių fondas auga' 18 Nov. 2002: 1; Baltutis 1983.

56 Kazokas 1992: 75.

57 *Australijos lietuvių metraštis* 1961: 91.

58 Pranauskas 2003 interviews, see Appendix 2.

## Chapter Three

1 Pranauskas 2003: 75; Baltutienė et al. 1990: 58.

2 Smith 1994: 121.

3 Pranauskas 2003 interviews, see Appendix 2.

4 Pranauskas 2003: 77; Migration in the 1970s was associated with the process of de-Stalinisation when fever restrictions on non-Russians took place. See Remeikis 1980: 37.

5 Pranauskas 2003 interviews, see Appendix 2.

6 Pranauskas 2003: 77; interviews, see Appendix 2.

7 Grant 1979: 25.

8 Kuzin 1972: 12–13; Jacoby 1975: 100; Matthews 1982: 101.

9 Pranauskas 2003: 79.

10 Ibid.; interviews, see Appendix 2.

11 Pranauskas 2003 interviews, see Appendix 2.

12 Pranauskas 2003: 80; interviews, see Appendix 2.

13 Pranauskas 2003: 80.

14 Ibid.: 81; interviews, see Appendix 2.

15 Pranauskas 2003 interviews, see Appendix 2.

16 Ibid.

17 Ibid.

18 Ibid.

19 Ibid.

20 Ibid.

21 Ibid.

22 Ibid.

23 Ibid.

24 Vardys 1978: 72.

25 Mayakovsky in Smith 1990: 195.

26 Pranauskas 2003: 84; interview, see Appendix 2.

27 Pranauskas 2003 interview, see Appendix 2.

28 Pranauskas 2003: 85; interviews, see Appendix 2.

29 Pranauskas 2003 interviews, see Appendix 2; Krickus 1997: 25.

30 Pranauskas 2003 interview, see Appendix 2.

31 Pranauskas 2003: 86–8; interviews, see Appendix 2.

32 Ibid.

33 Pranauskas 2003 interview, see Appendix 2.

34 Ibid.

35 Juodytė 2002: 4, 15.

36 Pranauskas 2003: 86.

37 Dambrauskienė 2005: 5.

38 Varnas 22 Jan. 2001: 1, 3.

## Chapter Four

1 Pranauskas 2003: 74.

2 Ibid.: 94.

3 Ibid.: 95.

4 Pranauskas 2003 interviews, see Appendix 2.

5 Ibid.

6 Ibid.

7 Ibid.

8 Ibid.

9 Pranauskas 2003: 97.

10 Pranauskas 2003 interviews, see Appendix 2.

11 Pranauskas 2003: 51; interviews, see Appendix 2.

12 Pranauskas 2003 interview, see Appendix 2.

13 Ibid.; on earlier Lithuanian settlers in Australia see *Australijos lietuvių metraštis* 1961: 8–11 & Popenhagen 2012: 8–26.

14 Pranauskas 2003 interview, see Appendix 2.

15 Ibid.

16 Ibid.

17 Pranauskas 2003: 100; Pranauskas 2003 interviews, see Appendix 2; Baltutienė et al. 1990: 58.

18 Pranauskas 2003 interviews, see Appendix 2.

19 Pranauskas 2003: 100, 102; Pranauskas 2003 interviews, see Appendix 2.

20 Pranauskas 2003 interviews, see Appendix 2.

21 Ibid.

22 Žemkalnis in Šeštokas 2000: 8; Pranauskas 2003.

23 Vegys 3 Dec. 2001: 2.

24 Malijauskienė 6 Nov. 2000: 4.

25 Kabaila 29 Jan. 2001: 7; Kabaila 5 Feb. 2001: 7; Baltušytė 22 Jan. 2001: 2.

26 Zake 2010: 30.

27 Brah 1998: 20.

28 Pranauskas 2003 interview, see Appendix 2.

29 Ibid.

30 Pranauskas 2003: 112; interview, see Appendix 2.

31 Pranauskas 2003 interviews, see Appendix 2.

32 Ibid.

## Chapter Five

1 Zinkevičius 1993: 9.

2 Thurston in Paliokas 2011: 1.

3 Barclay 1951: 3.

4 Tarvydas 1997: 24.

5 Musgrave et al. 1973: 5–6.

6 See Tarvydas 1997: 38–40.

7 Derrida 1997: 115.

8 *Australijos lietuvių metraštis* 1961: 142, 230, 178, 202, 198; Clyne 1991: 16.

9 Pranauskas 1998 interview, see Appendix 1.

10 Musgrave et al. 1973: 5–6.

11 Baltutis 1983: 282.

12 Smolicz 1982: 1–15.

13 Smolicz 1983: 7–8.

14 Pranauskas 2003 interview, see Appendix 2.

15 Stephen in Metherell 1989: 1.

16 Taškūnas 2005: 23–4.

17 Didžienė 14 July 1997: 3.

18 Haugen in Clyne 1991: 91; Pranauskas 2003: 62.

19 Pranauskas 2003: 61–2, 64.

20 Kviecinskas 2002: 7.

21 Liubinienė 9 Jan. 2002: 1, 6.

22 Pranauskas 2003: 89–90.

23 Ibid.: 90.

24 Ibid.: 91; interview, see Appendix 2.

25 Pranauskas 2003 interview, see Appendix 2.

26 Ibid.

27 Taškūnas 1998: 11, 46–7.

28 Ambrazevičius 1996: 5.

29 Chatterji 2011: 62;

30 Ambrazevičius 1996: 5. Andriejauskaitė 1994: 15; 1998: 53.

31 Mikulskienė 2000.

32 Tarvydas 1997: 8; Mieldažys 1961: 24; Pranauskas 1998: 89–90.

33 Baltutienė et al. 1990: 64–94.

34 Pranauskas 1998: 45; Kazokas 1996: 53–6.

35 Juška 10 March 1969: 3.

36 Šimkus 23 April 1973: 1.

37 Pranauskas 1998: 52–6.

38 Pranauskas 1998 interview, see Appendix 1.

39 Budriūnas 1976: 2.

40 Baltutienė et al. 1990: 58.

41 Ibid.

# Appendices

## 1. Interviews conducted for Bachelor of Arts (BA) (Honours) thesis 'Fifty years of Lithuanian culture in Australia 1940s–1990s' (1998)

Face-to-face interview with P1, 20 August 1998, Adelaide

Face-to-face interview with P2, 19 May 1998, Melbourne

Telephone interview with P3, 28 June 1998, Hobart

Face-to-face interview with P4, 29 August 1998, Adelaide

## 2. Interviews conducted for Master of Arts (MA) thesis 'National and cultural identity in Australia: a study of Australian Lithuanians' (2003)

### *Postwar interviewees*

Face-to-face interview with P1, 23 May 2000, Melbourne

Face-to-face interview with P2, 15 May 2000, Sydney

Face-to-face interview with P3, 18 June 2000, Melbourne

Interview via email followed by telephone conversation with P4, 5 April 2000, Melbourne

Face-to-face interview with P5, 6 May 2000, Melbourne

Face-to-face interview with P6, 14 May 2000, Sydney

Face-to-face interview with P7, 15 May 2000, Sydney

Face-to-face interview with P8, 19 May 2000, Adelaide

Face-to-face interview with P9, 16 May 2000, Adelaide

Face-to-face interview with P10, 18 May 2000, Adelaide

Face-to-face interview with P11, 20 May 2000, Adelaide

Face-to-face interview with P12, 18 May 2000, Adelaide

Interview via post followed by telephone conversation with P13, 10 April 2000, Hobart

Interview via post followed by telephone conversation with P14, 17 April 2000, Geelong

Face-to-face interview with P15, 2 June 2000, Melbourne

Face-to-face interview with P16, 15 May 2000, Sydney

Face-to-face interview with P17, 16 May 2000, Sydney

Interview via post followed by telephone conversation with P18, 17 April 2000, Geelong

Interview via post followed by telephone conversation with P19, 26 April 2000, Canberra

Face-to-face interview with P20, 21 May 2000, Adelaide

Face-to-face interview with P21, 18 July 2000, Melbourne

Face-to-face interview with P22, 15 May 2000, Sydney

Face-to-face interview with P23, 15 May 2000, Sydney

Face-to-face interview with P24, 18 May 2000, Adelaide

### *Recently arrived interviewees*

Interview via email with R1, 12 June 2000, Melbourne
Face-to-face interview with R2, 24 June 2000, Melbourne
Face-to-face interview with R3, 24 June 2000, Melbourne
Interview via post with R4, 2 May 2000, Melbourne
Face-to-face interview with R5, 26 May 2000, Melbourne
Face-to-face interview with R6, 20 May 2000, Adelaide
Face-to-face interview with R7, 23 July 2000, Melbourne
Interview via post with R8, 26 April 2000, Melbourne
Interview via post with R9, 11 May 2000, Adelaide
Interview via post with R10, 10 May 2000, Geelong
Face-to-face interview with R11, 21 May 2000, Adelaide
Interview via post with R12, 12 May 2000, Adelaide
Face-to-face interview with R13, 20 May 2000, Adelaide
Face-to-face interview with R14, 20 May 2000, Adelaide
Face-to-face interview with R15, 14 May 2000, Sydney
Face-to-face interview with R16, 13 May 2000, Sydney
Face-to-face interview with R17, 13 May 2000, Sydney
Face-to-face interview with R18, 23 July 2000, Melbourne
Interview via e-mail with R19, 12 June 2000, Melbourne
Face-to-face interview with R20, 15 May 2000, Sydney
Interview via post with R21, 2 June 2000, Geelong

### *Australian-born interviewees*

Face-to-face interview with D1, 21 May 2000, Adelaide
Face-to-face interview with D2, 13 May 2000, Sydney
Face-to-face interview with D3, 15 May 2000, Adelaide
Face-to-face interview with D4, 18 May 2000, Adelaide
Face-to-face interview with D5, 18 May 2000, Melbourne
Face-to-face interview with D6, 2 June 2000, Melbourne
Face-to-face interview with D7, 20 May 2000, Adelaide

## 3. A note on methodology

As part of my MA thesis, in order to investigate differences in attitudes and behaviour between postwar Lithuanians, their descendants, and more recent Lithuanian migrants, I considered gathering data by representative sampling. This was a difficult task as I had no means of contacting all Lithuanians in Australia. Community lists were incomplete and out of date. Selecting Lithuanian surnames from telephone directories was deemed to be unreliable because of the possibility of surname changes due to either preference or marriage. Having few other options, in October 1999–January 2000, using the outdated community registry as a guide, I distributed a questionnaire to the leaders of the different Australian Lithuanian organisations in Melbourne, Sydney, Adelaide, Geelong and Hobart. The leaders of these groups passed the questionnaire on to their members. Also, I distributed my questionnaire to more recently arrived Lithuanians who I either personally knew or found out about through word of mouth. Thus, the immediate postwar arrivals and descendants sampled here are primarily drawn from the population of Lithuanians who, to a greater or lesser degree, participate in the Australian Lithuanian community, though some non-participants have been included to give a fuller picture. The sample is not representative of all persons of Lithuanian descent living in Australia. However, in relation to the immediate postwar migrants and their descendants, my interest is mainly in ethnicity maintenance or the 'preservation' (rather than the loss) of Lithuanianness. Therefore, a survey of community participants is appropriate and consistent with the overall aim of this study. However, the more recent arrivals surveyed are more diverse. As I am interested in the experiences and attitudes of the newer arrivals irrespective of their local Lithuanian community participation status, I have sought to obtain a wider variety of respondents within this group than would be possible from relying on community organisation lists alone.

Of 396 questionnaires distributed, 172 completed questionnaires were returned, giving a response rate of 43 per cent. Of those who responded, 53 per cent were postwar migrants, 26 per cent recent migrants, and 19 per cent were descendants of postwar migrants, and 2 per cent did not specify their year of arrival in Australia.

After the questionnaire results were analysed, a subsample was selected for more in-depth interviews – the purpose being to gain a richer qualitative picture of the thoughts and experiences of Lithuanians in Australia. I did this by contacting 82 randomly selected questionnaire respondents. Between April–July 2000 open-ended face-to-face interviews took place in Sydney, Adelaide and Melbourne. Some of these interviews were further followed by the telephone conversations. Interviews with participants in Geelong, Hobart and Canberra were conducted by post. Participants who were not available for face-to-face or telephone interviews were sent interview questions, which were returned by either email or post. Some of them were further contacted by telephone for extended discussion about their answers. The numbers of participants were: 42 postwar Lithuanians, 23 recent arrivals and 17 descendants of postwar Lithuanians. Although all interviewees gave their written permission to use information from their interviews, some of them felt uncomfortable about their names being revealed. For this reason, names have been replaced by letters and numbers, with the first letter identifying interviewees which group interviewees belong to as follows: P (postwar migrant), R (recent migrant), and D (descendant of postwar migrant). Individuals within each subgroup are identified by numbers. Thus, P1 is the unique identifier of one of the respondents within the postwar migrant group. Information about the survey participants mentioned in this book is provided in Appendices 1 and 2.

While the above samples might not be a statistically accurate reflection of the total Lithuanian community, a diverse range of respondents (gender, different ages, various geographical locations, educational background etc.) have been surveyed and interviewed. While all the important demographic subgroups might not be represented exactly in the proportions in which they are found in the community, I can confidently assert that all the major subgroups are represented and have been given a voice.

# Bibliography

As well as the references listed in the Notes, information for these chapters has been obtained from other references, all of which are listed below.

## Introduction

Baltutis, Monica (1981). *Lithuanians in Melbourne 1947–1980*, BA Honours Thesis, Department of History, University of Melbourne, Melbourne.

Baskauskas, Liucija (1985). *An urban enclave: Lithuanian refugees in Los Angeles*, AMS Press, New York.

Bhabha, Homi (1993). *The location of culture*, Routledge, London.

Brah, Avtar (1998). *Cartographies of diaspora: contesting identities*, Routledge, London & New York.

Clifford, James (1994). 'Diasporas', *Cultural Anthropology*, vol. 9, no. 3, pp. 302–38.

Eckermann, Ann-Katrin (1994). *One classroom, many cultures: teaching strategies for culturally different children*, Allen & Unwin, London.

*Gallup polls* (1947), viewed 9 Nov. 2012, <http://trove.nla.gov.au/newspaper/result?q=gallup+polls+1947%2B>.

Hall, Stuart (1990). 'Cultural identity in diaspora', in Rutherford, Jonathan (ed.), *Identity: community, culture, difference*, Laurence & Wishalt, London, pp. 222–37.

Hall, Stuart (1993). 'Culture, community, nation', *Cultural Studies*, vol. 7, no. 3, pp. 349–63.

Hall, Stuart, Held, David & McGrew, Tony (eds.) (1992). *Modernity and its futures,* Polity Press, Cambridge.

Mishra, Vijay (ed.) (Nov. 1992–May 1993). 'Introduction', *Span*, Diasporas, double issues no. 34–35, pp. 1–2.

Pranauskas, Grazina (1998). 'Fifty years of Lithuanian culture in Australia 1940s–1990s', BA Honours Thesis, Deakin University, Geelong.

– – (2003). 'National and cultural identity in diaspora: a study of Australian Lithuanians', MA Dissertation, Deakin University, Geelong.

Putniņš, Aldis L (1981). *Latvians in Australia: alienation and assimilation,* Australian National University Press, Canberra.

Rutherford, Jonathan (ed.) (1990). 'The third space: interview with Homi Bhabha', in *Identity: community, culture, difference*, Lawrence & Wishart, London, pp. 207–21.

Safran, William (1991). 'Diasporas in modern societies: myths of homeland and return', *Diaspora*, vol. 1, no. 1, pp. 83–99.

Senn, Alfred Erick (1995). *Gorbachev's failure in Lithuania,* St Martin's Press, New York.

Taškūnas, Algimantas P (2005). *Lithuanian studies in Australia*, Tasmania University Union Lithuanian Studies Society, Hobart.

Walker, Conner (1986). 'The impact on homelands upon diasporas', in Sheffer, Gabriel (ed.), *Modern diasporas in international politics*, Croom Helm, London & Sydney, pp. 16–46.

## Chapter 1

Anderson, Benedict, new edn. (2006) [1983]. *Imagined communities: reflections on the origin and spread of nationalism*, Verso, London & New York.

Andriejauskaitė, Aurelija (ed.) (1994). *Dainų diena, pasaulio lietuvių dainų šventė Lietuva 1994* (Song day, world Lithuanian song festival Lithuania 1994), Lietuvių Liaudies Kultūros Centras, Vilnius.

Andriejauskaitė, Aurelija (ed.) (1998). *Dainų diena, pasaulio lietuvių dainų šventė* (Song day, world Lithuanian song festival), Petro Offsetas, Vilnius.

Astrauskas, Ramūnas (28 April 2003). '"Trečioji banga" – JAV Valstijose' (The 'third wave' - United States of America), *Mūsų Pastogė,* no. 16, p. 4.

Bethell, Nicholas (1974). *The last secret: the delivery to Stalin of over two million Russians by Britain and the United States,* Basic Books, New York.

Birn, Ruth Bettina (2006). *Die sicherheitspolizei in Eastland 1941–1944: eine studie zur collaboration im Osten*, Ferdinand Schöningh, Paderborn.

Birškys, Betty, Birškys, Antanas, Putniņš Aldis L & Salasoo, Inno (1986). *The Baltic peoples: Lithuanians Latvians Estonians in Australia,* Australian Ethnic Heritage Series, AE Press, Melbourne.

Boyce, Peter (2010). 'The reversal of Whitlam's recognition', *Lithuanian Papers*, no. 24, pp. 34–5.

Brazytė-Bindokienė, Danutė (1989). *Lietuvių papročiai ir tradicijos išeivijoje* (Lithuanian customs and traditions in diaspora), Pasaulio Lietuvių Bendruomenė, Chicago, Illinois.

Budreckis, Algirdas (1969). 'Lithuanian resistance, 1940–52', in Gerutis, Albertas (ed.), *Lithuania 700 Years*, Manyland Books, New York, pp. 313–92.

Dapkutė, Daiva (Fall 2012). 'An overview of the emigration processes of Lithuanians', *Lituanus*, vol. 58, no. 3, pp. 5–29.

Daugirdaitė-Sruogienė, Vanda (1990). *Lietuvos istorija* (Lithuanian history), Vyturys, Vilnius.

Dawisha, Karen & Parrott, Bruce (1995). *Russia and the new states of Euroasia: the political upheaval*, Cambridge University Press, Melbourne.

Dunsdorfs, Edgars (1975). *The Baltic dilemma: the case of the de jure recognition by Australia of the incorporation of the Baltic states into the Soviet Union*, part 1, Robert Speller and Sons, New York.

Dunsdorfs, Edgars (1982). *The Baltic dilemma: the case of the de jure recognition by Australia of the incorporation of the Baltic states into the Soviet Union*, part 2, Baltic Council of Australia, Melbourne.

Gerutis, Albertas (ed.) (1969). Budreckis, Algirdas, trans, *Lithuania 700 years,* Manyland Books, New York.

Gellately, Robert (2007). *Lenin, Stalin, and Hitler: the age of social catastrophe,* Alfred A. Knopf, New York.

Gierowski, Józef Andrzej (1986). *Historia Polski 1764–1864* (History of Poland 1764–1864), Państwowe Wydawnictwo Naukowe (Polish Scientific Publishers PWN), Warszawa.

Giordano, Christian (1997). 'Lex talionis: citizens and stateless in the Baltic states', *Anthropological Journal on European Cultures*, vol. 6, no. 1, pp. 101–23.

Gordon, Ellen J (1996). 'The revival of Polish national consciousness: a comparative study of Lithuania, Belarus, and Ukraine', *Nationalities Papers,* vol. 24, no. 2, pp. 217–36.

Gross, Jan T (1988). *Revolution from abroad*, Princeton University Press, New Jersey, pp. 161–2.

Hall, Stuart, David, Held and Tony, McGrew (eds.) (1992). *Modernity and its futures,* Polity Press, Cambridge.

Hope, Nicholas (1994). 'Interwar statehood: symbol and reality', in Smith, Graham (ed.), *The Baltic states: the national self-determination of Estonia, Latvia and Lithuania,* St Martin's Press, New York, pp. 41–68.

Hosking, Geoffrey, Aves, Jonathan & Duncan, Peter (eds.) (1992). *The road to post-communism: independent political movements in the Soviet Union, 1985–1991,* Pinter Publishers, New York.

Hroch, Miroslav (1996). 'From national movement to the fully-formed nation: the nation building process in Europe', in Eley, Geoff & Suny, Ronald Grigor (eds.), *Becoming national: a reader*, Oxford University Press, Oxford & New York, pp. 60–77.

Jakštas, Juozas (1969). 'Lithuania to World War One', in Gerutis, Albertas (ed.), Budreckis, Algirdas trans, *Lithuania 700 Years,* Manyland Books, New York, pp. 43–144.

Johannsen, Lars & Pedersen, Karen Hilmer (Sep. 2011). 'The institutional roots of anti-corruption policies: comparing the three Baltic states', *Journal of Baltic Studies*, Routledge, vol. 42, no. 3, pp. 329–46.

Jupp, James (1995). *Immigration: Australian perspectives,* Walker, David (ed.), Oxford University Press, Melbourne.

Kangeris, Kārlis (2006). 'German plans for retreat from the Baltics: the Latvian case', in Kumer-Haukanõmm, Kaja, Rosenberg, Tiit & Tammaru, Tiit (eds.), *Suur põgenemine 1944: Eest lahkumine läände ja selle mõjud*, Tartu Ülikooli Kirjastus, Tartu, pp. 39–49.

Kasekamp, Andres (2010). *A history of the Baltic states*, Palgrave, Macmillan, London & New York.

Kazokas, Genovaitė (1992). *Lithuanian artists in Australia 1950–1990*, PhD Thesis, University of Tasmania, Hobart.

Kiaupa, Zigmantas (2005). *The history of Lithuania*, Baltos Lankos, Vilnius.

Knight, John (1979). 'The Baltic states: foreign policy and domestic response, 1974–78', *The Australian Journal of Politics and History,* p. 35.

Kramer, Mark (2009). 'The dialectics of empire: Soviet leaders and the challenge of civil resistance in East-Central Europe, 1968–91', in Roberts, Adam & Garton Ash, Timothy (eds.), *Civil resistance and power politics: the experience of non-violent action from Gandhi to the present*, Oxford University Press.

Krickus, Richard J (1997). *Showdown: the Lithuanian rebellion and the breakup of the Soviet empire*, Brassey's, Washington & London.

Kudirka, Juozas (1991). *The Lithuanians: an ethnic portrait,* Lithuanian Folk Culture Centre, Vilnius.

Kudirka, Simas & Eichel, Larry (1978). *For those still at sea: the defection of the Lithuanian sailor,* The DialPress, New York.

Kunz, Egon F (1988). *Displaced persons: Calwell's new Australians,* Australian National University Press, Canberra.

Kumer-Haukanõmm, Kaja (2009). 'Eestlaste põgenemine Saksamaale', in Hallik, Terje, Kull, Kristi & Laidla, Janet (eds.), *Eestlaste põgenemine läände teise maailmasõja ajal,* Korp! Filiae Patriae, Tartu, pp. 13–53.

*Lietuva: dokumentai, liudijimai, atgarsiai, 1991.01.13* (Documents, witnessing, comments 1991.01.13) (1991). Spaudos Departamentas, Vilnius.

*Lietuva: dokumentai, liudijimai, atgarsiai, 1991.01.13, papildymai* (Documents, witnessing, comments 1991.01.13, additions) (1991). Spaudos Departamentas, Vilnius.

'Lietuvoje sumažėjo gyventojų' (Lithuania is losing its population), (30 Nov. 2002), ELTA, *Klaipėda,* p. 5.

*Lietuvos TSR istorija, nuo seniausių laikų iki 1917 metų* (Soviet Lithuanian history from ancient times to 1917) 2nd edn. (1986). vol. 1. (Transcript of original translation can be found on Senieji lietuviški raštai (Old Lithuanian texts)), viewed 25 Jan. 2013, <http://lietuvos.istorija.net/lituanistica/1791-05-03.htm>.

*Lietuvių enciklopedija* (Lithuanian encyclopedia) (1955). vol. 5, Spaudos fondas, Boston.

Lithuanian Bureau of Statistics: 'Population at the beginning of the year by ethnicity, statistical indicator and year', viewed 2 Jan. 2013, <http://db1.stat.gov.lt/statbank/selectvarval/saveselections.asp?MainTable=M3010215&PLanguage=1&TableStyle=&Buttons=&PXSId=3236&IQY=&TC=&ST=ST&rvar0=&rvar1=&rvar2=&rvar3=&rvar4=&rvar5=&rvar6=&rvar7=&rvar8=&rvar9=&rvar10=&rvar11=&rvar12=&rvar13=&rvar14=>.

Mackevičius, Mečislovas (1986). 'Lithuanian resistance to German mobilisation attempts 1941–1944', *Lituanus,* vol. 32, no. 4, pp. 1–7, viewed 20 Jan. 2012, <http://www.lituanus.org/1986/86_4_02.htm>.

Märtson, Tonis (2011). 'Recognition of annexation of the Baltic states by Australia', *Ajalooline Ajakiri, no. 1, vol. 135,* pp. 65–84.

Matulionis, Arvydas (1992). 'Nationalism and the process of state-building in Lithuania', *Sisyphus,* vol. 8, no. 2, pp. 121–4.

Mole, Richard C.M. (2012). *The Baltic states from the Soviet Union to the European Union: identity, discourse and power in the post-communist transition of Estonia, Latvia and Lithuania*, Routledge, Taylor & Francis Group, London & New York.

Nogee, Joseph, L (ed.) (1972). *Man, state, and society in the Soviet Union*, Praeger Publishers, New York.

Öpik, Paul, Tündern-Smith, Ann (8 Feb. 2006), 'A recognition timeline for Whitlam's agreement to de jure recognition of the Soviet occupation of the Baltic states', *Meie Kodu*.

Öpik, Paul, Tündern-Smith, Ann (22 Feb. 2006). 'Renouf's role in recognition: foreign affairs head was key player, wanted history to recognise him!' *Meie Kodu*.

Pranauskas, Grazina (2003). 'National and cultural identity in diaspora: a study of Australian Lithuanians', MA, Deakin University, Geelong.

Putrimas, Edis (2001). 'Emigracinės bangos iš Lietuvos' (Waves of emigration from Lithuania), *Mūsų Pastogė*, no. 1–2, 15 Jan., pp. 5, 10.

Puzinas, Juozas (1969). 'The origins of the Lithuanian nation', in Gerutis, Albertas (ed.), Budreckis, Algirdas, trans, *Lithuania 700 years*, Manylands Books, New York, pp. 1–42.

*Radio Free/Radio Liberty*, in Putrimas, Edis (15 Jan. 2001). 'Emigracinės bangos iš Lietuvos' (Waves of emigration from Lithuania), *Mūsų Pastogė*, no. 1-2, pp. 5, 10.

Raštikis, Stasys (1982). *Lietuvos likimo kelias* (Lithuanian road of fate), Akademinė Skautijos Leidykla, Chicago.

Reinans, Alur (2006). 'Eesti põgenikud Rootsi statistikas', in Kumer-Haukanõmm, Kaja, Rosenberg, Tiit & Tammaru, Tiit (eds.), *Suur põgenemine 1944: Eest lahkumine läände ja selle mõjud*, Tartu Ülikooli Kirjastus, Tartu, pp. 122–46.

Remeikis, Thomas (1980). *Opposition to the Soviet rule in Lithuania 1945–1980*, Institute of Lithuanian Studies Press, Chicago, Illinois.

Renouf, Alan (1979). *The frightened country*, The Macmillan Co. of Australia, Melbourne.

Riasanovsky Nicholas V, 5th edn. (1993) [1963]. *A history of Russia*, Oxford, California, New York.

Rose, Barrie (1992). 'The historical background of Lithuanian freedom', in Taškūnas, P. Algimantas (ed.), *Lithuania in 1991*, Lithuanian Studies Society, T.U.U. Hobart, pp. 11–19.

Rose, Richard, Mishler, William & Haerpfer, Christian (1998). *Democracy and its alternatives: understanding post-communist societies*, Polity Press, Cambridge.

Rubas, Jurgis (1992). 'Lithuania in 1991', in Taškūnas, Algimantas P (ed.), *Lithuania in 1991*, Sandy Bay, Tasmania, Lithuanian Studies Society, T.U.U, Hobart, pp. 26–42.

Saldukas, Linas (2006). 'Lithuanians in DP camps in Germany', in Kumer-Haukanõmm, Kaja, Rosenberg, Tiit & Tammaru, Tiit (eds.) *Suur põgenemine 1944: Eest lahkumine läände ja selle mõjud*, Tartu Ülikooli Kirjastus, Tartu, pp. 52–68.

Samoškaitė, Eglė (7 March 2012). 'Viena iš nusivylimo priežasčių' (One of the reasons for disappointment), *Mūsų Pastogė*, no. 9, pp. 4-7.

Senn, Alfred Erick (1995). *Gorbachev's failure in Lithuania,* St Martin's Press, New York.

– – (1997). 'Lithuania: rights and responsibilities of independence', in Bremmer, Ian & Ray, Taras (eds.), *New states new politics: building the post-Soviet nations*, Cambridge University Press, New York, pp. 353–75.

– – (2007). *Lithuania 1940: revolution from above. On the boundary of two worlds: identity, freedom and moral imagination in the Baltics,* Ropodi, Amsterdam.

Shtromas, Aleksandras (1994). 'The Baltic states as Soviet republics: tensions and contradictions', in Smith, Graham (ed.), *The Baltic states: the national self-determination of Estonia, Latvia and Lithuania,* St Martin's Press, New York, pp. 86–117.

Shuey, Madeleine (2004). *Australia's 1974 recognition, de jure, of Soviet sovereignty in the Baltic states,* B.A. Honours thesis, University of Tasmania, Hobart.

Shuey, Madeleine (2004). 'The quest for the truth', *Lithuanian Papers,* no.18, vo. 2044, pp. 57–9.

Smith, Graham (ed.) (1994). *The Baltic states: the national self-determination of Estonia, Latvia and Lithuania*, St Martins Press, New York.

Snyder, Timothy (2004). *The reconstruction of nations: Poland, Ukraine, Lithuania, Belarus, 1569–1999,* Yale University Press, New Haven, Connecticut.

Solzhenitsyn, Alexander (1974) [1973]. *The Gulag Archipelago 1918-1957,* Collins/Fontana, Wilke & Co Ltd, Melbourne.

Straukas, Bronius (1983). 'Lithuanians in Australia', in Baltutis, Viktoras (ed.), *Australijos lietuvių metraštis*, S. A. Print, Adelaide, pp. 9–21.

Sužiedėlis, Saulius (2011). *Historical dictionary of Lithuania*, Scarecrow Press, London.

Tarvydas, Ramūnas (1997). *From amber coast to apple tree: fifty years of Baltic immigrants in Tasmania 1948–1998,* Baltic Semicentennial Commemoration Activities Organising Committee, Hobart.

Taškūnas, Algimantas P (ed.) (1992). *Lithuania in 1991*, T.U.U. Lithuanian Studies Society, Sandy Bay, Hobart.

Taškūnas, Algimantas P (29 Sep. 2012). 'The 1974 Baltic decision revised', 16th AABC Conference paper, University of Melbourne, Melbourne.

*The chronicle of the Catholic Church in Lithuania* (19 Nov. 1972). no. 1, viewed 3 Nov. 2012, <http://www.lkbkronika.lt/en/index.php?option=com_content&view=article&id=342:the-chronicle-of-the-catholic-church-in-lithuania&catid=34:frontpage&Itemid=227>.

Thom, Françoise & Regan, David (1988). *Glasnost, Gorbachev & Lenin: behind the new thinking*, Polity Research Publications, London.

Thurston, Theodore S (2011). *Lithuanian language*, in Paliokas, Eugenijus, viewed 3 June 2012, <http://paliokas.blogspot.com.au/2011/07/lithuanian-language.html>

Truska, Liudas, Anušauskas, Arvydas & Petravičiūtė, Inga (1999). *Sovietinis saugumas Lietuvoje 1940–1953 metais* (Soviet life in Lithuania 1940–1953), MGB–KGB agencies in occupied Lithuania, pp. 99–102, viewed 2 June 2012, <http://www.genocid.lt/centras/lt/1498/a/>.

Urban, William (1992). 'Implications of the past for the future of the Baltic states', in Taškūnas, Algimantas P (ed.) (1992). *Lithuania in 1991*, Sandy Bay, Tasmania, Lithuanian Studies Society, T.U.U, Hobart, pp. 144–55.

Urbonaitė, Audronė (6 Jan. 2002). 'Antano Sniečkaus mitas' (Myth of Antanas Sniečkus), Ekstra, no.1, p. 213

Varnas, Saulius (17 Oct. 2012). 'SBS rodyto filmo 'Rewriting history' reikalu' (In response to a film 'Rewriting history' on SBS), *Mūsų Pastogė*, no. 41, p. 3.

Vardys, Vytas Stanley (ed.) (1965). *Lithuania under the Soviets: portrait of a nation, 1940–65,* Frederick A. Praeger, New York.

Vardys, Vytas Stanley (1978). *The Catholic Church: dissent and nationality in Soviet Lithuania*, East European Quarterly, Boulder, New York.

Vardys, Vytas Stanley & Sedaitis, Judith B (1997). *Lithuania: the rebel nation,* Westview Series on the Post-Soviet Republics, WestviewPress, Colorado.

*Vilmorus* (16 Sep. 2002). in 'Jaunuomenė norėtų iškeliauti iš Lietuvos' (The youth would like to leave Lithuania), *Mūsų Pastogė*, no. 37, p. 4.

Waldren, Stephen (1993). *Lithuania: the impact of the Stimson doctrine,* Sandy Bay, TUU Lithuanian Studies Society, Hobart.

## Chapter 2

*Australijos lietuvių metraštis* (The Australian Lithuanian annual chronicle) (1961). Australian Lithuanian Community's weekly *Mūsų Pastogė*, Sydney.

Appleyard, Reginals Thomas (1972). 'Immigration and national development', in Roberts, Hew (ed.), *Australian immigration policy*, University of Western Australia Press, Nedlands, Perth, pp. 13–28.

Baltutienė, Dana Maria, Baltrukonienė, Alisa ir Mulevičienė, Jadvyga, red. (1990). *Australijos lietuvių 40 metų kultūrinė veikla 1950–1990* (Forty years to the Australian Lithuanian cultural activities 1950–1990), Reflection Printing, Melbourne.

Baltutis, Viktoras (ed.) (1983). *Australijos lietuvių metraštis II* (The Australian Lithuanian annual chronicle II), Australian Lithuanian Community and Australian Lithuanian Foundation, Adelaide.

Bethell, Nicholas (1974). *The last secret: the delivery to Stalin of over two million Russians by Britain and the United States*, Basic Books, New York.

Birškys, Betty, Birškys, Antanas, Putniņš Aldis L & Salasoo, Inno (1986). *The Baltic peoples: Lithuanians Latvians Estonians in Australia,* Australian Ethnic Heritage Series, AE Press, Melbourne.

Birn, Ruth Bettina (2006). *Die sicherheitspolizei in Eastland 1941–1944: eine studie zur collaboration im Osten*, Ferdinand Schöningh, Paderborn.

Cohen, Steven M & Kapsis, Robert E (1977). 'Religion, ethnicity and party affiliation in the U.S.: evidence from pooled electoral surveys, 1968–72', *American Journal of Sociology*, vol. 56, no. 2, pp. 637–53.

Collins, Jock, 2nd edn. (1991) [1988]. 'From Bonegilla to Vietnamatta: Australia's postwar refugees, in Collins, Jock, *Migrant hands in a distant land, Australia's post-war migration*, Pluto Press, Leichardt, Sydney.

Dunsdorfs, Edgars (1975). *The Baltic dilemma: the case of the de jure recognition by Australia of the incorporation of the Baltic states into the Soviet Union,* Part 1, Robert Speller and Sons, New York.

Garrett, Stephen A (1978). 'Eastern European ethnic groups and American foreign policy', *Political Science Quarterly*, vol. 98, pp. 301–22.

Gellately, Robert (2007). *Lenin, Stalin, and Hitler: the age of social catastrophe*, Alfred A. Knopf, New York.

Ginsburgs, George (1957). 'The Soviet Union and the problem of refugees and displaced persons 1917–1956', *The American Journal of the International Law*, vol. 51, no. 353, pp. 354–8.

Holt, Harold (28 Jan. 1953). 'Baltic settlers in Australia', *Mūsų Pastogė*, p. 3.

*Immigration policies and Australia's population: a Green Paper* (1977). Australian Population and Immigration Council, Australian Government Publishing Services, Canberra.

Jupp, James (1995). *Immigration: Australian perspectives*, Walker, David (ed.), Oxford University Press, Melbourne.

Kamien, Max (2007). 'Overseas trained doctors', *Australian doctors trained overseas Association*, viewed 2 June 2012, < http://www.adtoa.org/index.pl?page=468>.

Kasekamp, Andres (2010). *History of the Baltic states*, Basingstoke, Palgrave, Macmillan.

Kazokas, Genovaitė (1992). *Lithuanian artists in Australia 1950–1990*, PhD Thesis, University of Tasmania, Hobart.

Krupinski, Jerzy (1976). 'Confronting theory with data: the case of suicide, drug abuse and mental illness in Australia', *Australian and New Zealand Journal of Sociology*, no. 12, pp. 91–100.

Krupinski, Jerzy, Stoller, Alan & Wallace, Lesley (1973). 'Psychiatric disorders in East European refugees now in Australia', *Social Science and Medicine*, vol. 7, pp. 31–49.

Kunz, Egon F (1988). *Displaced persons: Calwell's new Australians*, Australian National University Press, Canberra.

Kuzin, N.P. (1972). Glagoleva, Fainna, trans. *Education in the U.S.S.R*, Central Books, London.

L'Hommedieu, Jonathan H (2011). 'Exiles and constituents: Baltic refugees and American Cold War politics, 1948–1960', PhD dissertation, University of Turku, Turku.

'Lietuvių fondas auga' (Lithuanian foundation expands) (18 Nov. 2002). *Mūsų Pastogė*, no. 46, p. 1.

Plume, Ventis & Plume, John (eds.) (2004). *Insula: displaced persons assembly center: a Latvian memoir*, Kirk House Publishers, Minneapolis.

Pranauskas, Grazina (1988). 'Fifty years of Lithuanian culture in Australia 1940s–1990s', BA Honours, Deakin University, Geelong.

– – (2003). 'National and cultural identity in diaspora: a study of Australian Lithuanians', MA Dissertation, Deakin University, Geelong.

Putniņš, Aldis L (1981). *Latvians in Australia: alienation and assimilation,* Australian National University Press, Canberra.

Saidel, Rochelle (1984). *The outraged conscience: seekers of justice for Nazi war criminals in America*, State University of New York Press, Albany.

Straukas, Bronius (1983). 'Lithuanians in Australia', in Baltutis, Viktoras, red, *Australijos lietuvių metraštis II* (The Australian Lithuanian annual chronicle II), Australian Lithuanian Community and Australian Lithuanian Foundation, Adelaide, pp. 9–21.

Šeštokas, Josef (2010). *Welcome to little Europe: displaced persons and the North Camp*, Little Chicken Publishing, Sale.

Tarvydas, Ramūnas (1997). *From amber coast to apple tree: fifty years of Baltic immigrants in Tasmania 1948–1998,* Baltic Semicentennial Commemoration Activities Organising Committee, Hobart.

Taškūnas, Algimantas P (1980). 'Soviet/Australian dual citizenship', *Baltic News*, Feb/March, Hobart, pp. 5–8.

Zake, Ieva (2010). *American Latvians*, Transaction Publishers, New Brunswick & London.

Zubrickas, Boleslovas (1999). *Pasaulio lietuvių chorvedžiai* (World Lithuanian conductors), Enciklopedinis Žinynas, Lietuvos Liaudies Kultūros Centras, Vilnius, pp. 116–17, 302–3, 321–2, 427–8, 615–16.

## Chapter 3

Baltutienė, Dana Maria, Baltrukonienė, Alisa ir Mulevičienė, Jadvyga, red. (1990). *Australijos lietuvių 40 metų kultūrinė veikla 1950–1990* (Forty years to the Australian Lithuanian cultural activities 1950–1990), Reflection Printing, Melbourne.

Dambrauskienė, Jadvyga (20 March 2000). 'Mokytojai, susitikime' (Lets meet, teachers), *Mūsų Pastogė,* no. 11, p. 5.

Dunstan, John (1978). *Paths to excellence and the Soviet school*, NFER Publishing Company, Windsor.

Grant, Nigel, 4th edn. (1979) [1964]. *Soviet education,* Penguin Books, Harmondsworth, New York.

Jacoby, Susan (1975). *Inside Soviet schools*, Hill and Wang, New York.

Juodytė, Gražina (10 Aug. 2002). 'Liuda Mačernienė: Australijoje, skirtingai nei Lietuvoje, visi laikosi įstatymų' (Liuda Mačernienė: by comparison to Lithuania, everyone is following the Statute in Australia), *Klaipėda*, pp. 4, 15.

Krickus, Richard J (1997). *Showdown: the Lithuanian rebellion and the breakup of the Soviet empire*, Brassey's, Washington & London.

Kuzin, N.P. (1972). Glagoleva, Fainna, trans, *Education in the U.S.S.R.*, Central Books, London, p. 13.

*Lithuanian settler arrivals: financial years 1950–51 to 1999–2000, Department of Immigration and Multicultural Affairs* (DIMA), Cat. no. 2064.0 – CDATA Online, viewed 20 Oct. 2008, <http://www.abs.gov.au/census>.

Matthews, Mervyn (1982). *Education in the Soviet Union: policies and institutions since Stalin*, George Allen & Unwin, London.

Pranauskas, Grazina (2003). 'National and cultural identity in diaspora: a study of Australian Lithuanians', MA Dissertation, Deakin University, Geelong.

Remeikis, Thomas (1980). *Opposition to the Soviet rule in Lithuania 1945–1980*, Institute of Lithuanian Studies Press, Chicago, Illinois.

Smith, Graham (1990). *The new Russians*, Random House, New York.

Smith, Graham (ed.) (1994). *The Baltic states: the national self-determination of Estonia, Latvia and Lithuania*, St Martins Press, New York.

Vardys, Stanley Vytas (1978). *The Catholic Church: dissent and nationality in Soviet Lithuania*, East European Quarterly, Boulder, New York.

Varnas, Saulius (22 Jan. 2001). 'ALB krašto tarybos atstovų suvažiavimas Sydnėjuje' (Local Australian Lithuanian community council delegates' convention in Sydney), *Mūsų Pastogė,* no. 3, pp. 1, 3.

Vishnevsky, Anatoli & Zayonchkovskaya, Zhanna (1994). 'Emigration from the former Soviet Union: the fourth wave', in Fassmann, Heinz & Műnz, Rainer (eds.), *European migration in the late twentieth century: historical patterns, actual trends, and social implications,* Edward Elgar, IIASA, Luxembourg, pp. 239–59.

## Chapter 4

Australian Bureau of Statistics (2011). 'Language spoken at home by proficiency in spoken English/Language by sex', viewed 11 Nov. 2012, http://www.abs.gov.au/ausstats/abs@.nsf/lookup/2011.0.55.001Main%20 Features1122011

*Australijos lietuvių metraštis* (The Australian Lithuanian annual chronicle) (1961). Australijos Lietuvių bendruomenės savaitraštis *Mūsų Pastogė*, vol. 1, Sydney.

Baltušytė, Rita (22 Jan. 2001). 'Redakcijos skiltis' (The editorial column), *Mūsų Pastogė*, no. 3, p. 2.

Baltutienė, Dana Maria, Baltrukonienė, Alisa ir Mulevičienė, Jadvyga, red. (1990). *Australijos lietuvių 40 metų kultūrinė veikla 1950–1990* (Forty years to the Australian Lithuanian cultural activities 1950–1990), Reflection Printing, Melbourne.

Bhabha, Homi (1994). *The location of culture*, Routledge, London.

Brah, Avtar (1998). *Cartographies of diaspora: contesting identities*, Routledge, London and New York.

Kabaila, Algimantas (22 Jan. 2001). 'ALB vakar, šiandien ir rytoj' (Australian Lithuanian community yesterday, today and tomorrow), *Mūsų Pastogė*, no. 3, p. 7.

– – (29 Jan. 2001). 'ALB vakar, šiandien ir rytoj' (Australian Lithuanian community yesterday, today and tomorrow), *Mūsų Pastogė*, no. 4, p. 7.

– – (5 Feb. 2001). 'ALB vakar, šiandien ir rytoj' (Australian Lithuanian community yesterday, today and tomorrow), Mūsų Pastogė, no. 5, p. 7.

– – (12 Feb. 2001). 'ALB vakar, šiandien ir rytoj' (Australian Lithuanian community yesterday, today and tomorrow), *Mūsų Pastogė*, no. 6, p. 7.

Malijauskienė, Janina (6 Nov. 2000). 'Spaudos kūkaliai' (Weeds of the press), Mūsų Pastogė, no. 44, p. 4.

Popenhagen, Luda (2012). *Australian Lithuanians*, UNSW, Sydney.

Pranauskas, Grazina (2003). 'National and cultural identity in diaspora: a study of Australian Lithuanians', MA, Deakin University, Geelong.

Rutherford, Jonathan (ed.) (1990). 'The third space: interview with Homi Bhabha', in *Identity: community, culture, difference*, Lawrence & Wishart, London, pp. 207–21.

Šeštokas, Vytautas (31 Oct. 2000). 'Lietuviai bėga iš Lietuvos' (Lithuanians are running from Lithuania), *Tėviškės Aidai,* no. 43, p. 8.

Vegys, Petras (3 Dec. 2001). 'Kodėl neiname į klubą' (Why we don't attend the club?), *Mūsų Pastogė,* no. 48, p. 2.

Zake, Ieva (2010). *American Latvians*, Transaction Publishers, New Brunswick & London.

## Chapter 5

Ambrazevičius, Rytis (ed.) (1996). *Lithuanian roots, an overview of Lithuanian traditional culture*, Lithuanian National Cultural Centre, Vilnius.

Andriejauskaitė, Aurelija (ed.) (1994). *Dainų diena, pasaulio lietuvių dainų šventė, Lietuva 1994* (Song day, world Lithuanian song festival, Lithuania 1994), Lietuvių Liaudies Kultūros Centras, Vilnius.

– – (1998). *Dainų dainų diena, pasaulio lietuvių dainų šventė,* (Song day, world Lithuanian song festival), Petro Offsetas, Vilnius.

*Australijos lietuvių metraštis* (The Australian Lithuanian annual chronicle) (1961). Australian Lithuanian Community's weekly *Mūsų Pastogė*, Sydney.

Baltutienė, Dana Maria, Baltrukonienė, Alisa ir Mulevičienė, Jadvyga, red. (1990). *Australijos lietuvių 40 metų kultūrinė veikla 1950–1990* (Forty years to the Australian Lithuanian cultural activities 1950–1990), Reflection Printing, Melbourne.

Baltutis, Viktoras (ed.) (1983). *Australijos lietuvių metraštis II* (The Australian Lithuanian annual chronicle II), Australian Lithuanian Community and Australian Lithuanian Foundation, Adelaide.

Baltrūnas, Leonas (1 Jan. 1983). 'Dainų šventė' (Song festival), *Mūsų Pastogė*, p. 3.

Barclay, Esmond (15 Feb. 1951). 'How new Australians study English', *Mūsų Pastogė*, p. 3.

Budriūnas, Bronius (28 Aug. 1976). 'Daina yra lietuvių tautos stiprybės šaltinis ir kultūros išraiška' (Song is the Lithuanian national strength and cultural expression), *Tėviškės Aidai*, p. 2.

Chatterji, Suniti Kumar (2011). 'Records of the ancient Baltic culture', in *Balts and Arians in their Indo-European background*, Ch. 9, viewed 30 Jan. 2012, <http://www.vaidilute.com/books/chatterji/chatterji-09.html>.

Clyne, Michael (1991). 'Australia between monolingualism and multiculturalism', in Clyne, Michael (ed.), *Community, languages, the*

*Australian experience*, Cambridge University Press, New York, p. 16.

Daugirdaitė-Sruogienė, Vanda (1990). *Lietuvos istorija* (Lithuanian history), Vyturys, Vilnius.

Derrida, Jacques (1997). 'Community without community', in Caputo, John D (ed.), *Deconstruction in the nutshell, a conversation with Jacque Derrida*, Fortham University Press, New York.

Didžienė, Dalia (14 July 1997). 'Gintaro tautinių šokių grupė ruošiasi' (Folk dance group Gintaras prepares), *Mūsų Pastogė*, p. 3.

Galbally Report (1978). viewed 20 Feb. 2012, <http://www.multiculturalaustralia.edu.au/history/timeline/period/Multiculturalism-in-Practice/screen/2.The-Galbally-Strategy-for-migrant-settlement>.

Juška, Jonas (10 March 1969). 'Lietuvių dienose pabuvojus' (Attending Australian Lithuanian Days), *Mūsų Pastogė,* p. 3.

Kazokas, Vincas (1996). Čiužauskaitė, Ilona (ed.), Mūsų pastogė Australijoje (Our haven in Australia), Žurnalistikos leidykla, Vilnius.

Klimas, Antanas (Spring 1973). 'Baltic and Slavic revised', *Lituanus*, vol. 19, no. 1, pp. 1–8, viewed 3 June 2012, <http//www.lituanus.org/1973/73_1_02.htm>.

Kviecinskas, Paulius (25 March 2002). 'Melbourno "Džiugo" tunto stovykla' (Melbourne 'Džiugas' tuntas Camp), *Mūsų Pastogė*, no. 12, p. 7.

Lang, George (2002). *Entwisted tongues: comparative Creole literatures*, Rodopi, Amsterdam.

Liubinienė, Alė (9 Jan. 2002). 'Easter Island (Velykų sala)', *Tėviškės Aidai*, no. 1, p. 6.

Metherell, Mark (26 Jan. 1989). 'Review states, says Sir Ninian', *The Age*, p. 1.

Mieldažys, Kazys (1961). 'Pirmieji žingsniai Australijoje' (First steps in Australia) in *Australijos lietuvių metraštis* (The Australian Lithuanian annual chronicle) (1961). Australijos lietuvių bendruomenės savaitraštis Mūsų Pastogė, vol. 1, Sydney, pp. 64–8.

Mikulskienė, Ona (2000). Čiurlionio ansamblis 1940*1949 dienoraštis (Čiurlionis' Ensemble diary 1940*1949), Lietuvos muzikų rėmimo fondas, Vilnius.

Musgrave, Peter William (1973). 'The school and migrants', in Bullivant, Brian Milton (ed.), *Educating the migrant child, concepts and cases*, Modern Education Series, Angus & Robertson, Sydney, pp. 5–6.

Mykolaitis-Putinas, Vincas (24 April 1959). 'Lietuvių tauta ir jos kultūra' (Lithuanian nation and its culture), *Mūsų Pastogė*, p. 3.

Ozolins, Uldis (1988). 'Government language policy initiatives and the future of ethnic languages in Australia', *International Journal of the Sociology of Language*, no. 72, p. 118.

Pocius, Daina (14 July 1997). 'Dvikalbė lietuviška bendruomenė – realybė ar mitas?' (Bilingual Lithuanian community – reality or myth?), *Mūsų Pastogė*, p. 4.

Pranauskas, Grazina (1998). 'Fifty years of Lithuanian culture in Australia 1940s–1990s', BA Honours Thesis, Deakin University, Geelong.

– – (2003). 'National and cultural identity in diaspora: a study of Australian Lithuanians', MA Dissertation, Deakin University, Geelong.

Rizvi, Fazal (1989). *Migration, ethnicity & multiculturalism (multiculturalism: making policy for a polyethnic society)*, vol. c, Deakin University, Geelong.

Smolicz, Jerzy Jaroslaw (1982). 'Social systems in multicultural societies', in *International Journal of Sociology and Social Policy*, vol. 3, no. 3, pp. 1–15.

– – (3–8 July 1983). 'Multiculturalism and an overarching framework of values: educational resources to assimilation, interaction, and separatism in ethnically plural societies', Discussion Paper, 11th Conference Würzburg, Federal Republic of Peru, pp. 7–8.

– – (1991). *Australian diversity: language, a bridge or a barrier?* Linguistic pluralism and education in Australia, Centre for Intercultural Studies and Multicultural Education, Adelaide.

Šarkauskas, Jonas (9 July 2001). 'Australijos lietuvių dienos' (Australian Lithuanian Days), *Mūsų Pastogė*, no. 27, p. 5.

Šimkus, Vaclovas (23 April 1973). 'Dainų šventės Australijoje' (Song festivals in Australia), *Mūsų Pastogė*, p. 1.

Tarvydas, Ramūnas (1997). *From amber coast to apple tree: fifty years of Baltic immigrants in Tasmania 1948–1998*, Baltic Semicentennial Commemoration Activities Organising Committee, Hobart.

Taškūnas, Algimantas P (1998). *Nereikalingų svetimžodžių rinkinys* (Collection of unnecessary barbarisms), Lithuanian Studies Society, University of Tasmania, Hobart.

– – (2005). *Lithuanian studies in Australia*, Tasmania University Union Lithuanian Studies Society, Hobart.

Thurston, Theodore S (2011). *Lithuanian language*, in Paliokas, Eugenijus (ed.), viewed 3 June 2012, <http://paliokas.blogspot.com.au/2011/07/lithuanian-language.html>

Tideman, Harold (16 March 1972). 'Fine operatic singing', *The Advertiser*, Geelong.

Zinkevičius, Zigmas (1993). *Rytų Lietuva praeityje ir dabar* (North Lithuania's past and present), Mokslo ir enciklopedijų leidykla, Vilnius.

# Index

# About the Author

Grazina Pranauskas completed her Choral Conducting degree at the Academy of Music and Theatre in Vilnius, Lithuania. Since 1989 she has lived in Australia, where she obtained Bachelor of Arts Degree Majoring in Journalism and Literary studies (1997). In 1998 she was awarded Bachelor of Arts Honours Degree for her thesis 'Fifty years of Lithuanian culture in Australia 1940s–1990s' from the Deakin University, Geelong. In 2003 Grazina was awarded her Master of Arts (by Research) degree for 'National and cultural identity in diaspora: a study of Australian Lithuanians' from the Deakin University, Geelong. In 2015 she completed her PhD in Creative Writing at Victoria University, Melbourne.

www.ingramcontent.com/pod-product-compliance
Ingram Content Group UK Ltd.
Pitfield, Milton Keynes, MK11 3LW, UK
UKHW041638190726
13854UKWH00006B/2565

9 781925 801170